CW00956483

A Guide to English in the 21st Century

A Guide to English in the 21st Century

Godfrey Howard

Cartoons by Gray Jolliffe

Duckworth

For Lesley Howard
who also enjoys words

This edition first published in 2002 by
Gerald Duckworth & Co Ltd
61 Frith Street, London W1D 3JL
Tel: 020 7434 4242
Fax: 020 7434 4420
Email: inquiries@duckworth-publishers.co.uk
www.ducknet.co.uk

Original edition published by Pelham Books in 1985
under the title *A Guide to Good English in the 1980s*

Original edition © by Malcolm Saunders Publishing Ltd
and Savitri Books Ltd.

Text © 1985, 2002 by Godfrey Howard
Cartoons © 1985 by Gray Jolliffe

A catalogue record for this book is available
from the British Library.

ISBN 0 7156 3168 3

Typeset by Derek Doyle & Associates, Liverpool
Printed in Great Britain by
Creative Print and Design Wales, Ebbw Vale

Acknowledgements

I am grateful to the writers, broadcasters and editors in the UK and USA who offered suggestions. Special thanks go to Malcolm Saunders, Susie Saunders and Mrinalini Srivastava for lively and helpful discussions in Great Russell Street, Fiona Duncan for her insight and patience as an editor, Francesca Kay for research, Lesley Howard Languages for masterly editorial guidance, Françoise Legrand for help in so many ways, Gray Jolliffe for his 'linguistic' cartoons, and to Deborah Blake, editorial director at Duckworth, for intelligent and friendly hand-holding.

And I also express appreciation to the following persons and publishers for the use of short quotations from copyright material. Every effort has been made to trace the owners of the copyright of quotations used: if there are any accidental omissions or inaccuracies, please accept my apologies.

George Allen & Unwin: Frederick Bodmer, *The Loom of Language*. W.H. Allen: Leo Rosten, *The Joys of Yiddish*. Bantam Books, Inc.: Marshall McLuhan, *The Medium is the Massage*. BBC Publications: Robert Burchfield, *The Spoken Word*. Cambridge University Press: Jenny Cheshire, *A Question of Masculine Bias* (English Today). Jonathan Cape: Ivor Brown, *A Word in Your Ear. Selected Letters of Raymond Chandler*, © College Trustees Limited. Clarkson N. Potter, Inc.: reprinted from *An Almanac of Words at Play* by Willard R. Espy, © 1975, used by permission of Clarkson N. Potter, Inc. Andre Deutsch: Ogden Nash, *I Wouldn't Have Missed It*. Anthony Burgess, *Joysprick*. Faber and Faber: T.S. Eliot, *Four Quartets. Poets in Conversation with John Haffenden. Financial Times*: Tim Waterstone. Fontana Paperbacks: Jean Aitchison, *Language Change: Progress or Decay*? John Georgiadis, Leader of London Symphony Orchestra. *Guardian*: Jack Cross, *Spreading the Word. Guardian*: Barry Hugill, *We're All Middle-Class Now*. Hamish Hamilton: Philip Howard, *Words Fail Me*. Eric Partridge, *Usage and Abusage*. Hamish Hamilton: James Thurber, *The Collection*, © 1963. HMSO Books: *The Bullock Report. The Complete Plain Words*. Macmillan:

Brian Foster, *The Changing English Language*. Schools Council Project. Methuen, London: Jilly Cooper, *Class*. Thomas Nelson & Sons: Geoffrey Gorer, *Sex and Marriage in England Today*. *New Statesman*: Vernon Scannell, *Protest Poem*. *New York Times*: William Safire, William Connolly. *Observer*: James Thurber, letter to Lewis Gannett, Robert McCrum, *They're Talking Our Language*, V.S. Naipaul. Paladin Books: Paul Robinson, *The Sexual Radicals*. Routledge & Kegan Paul: C.G. Jung, *The Structure and Dynamics of the Psyche*. Bernice Rubens, novelist and playwright. Secker and Warburg: Germaine Greer, *Sex and Destiny*. Advertisement for the *Times Literary Supplement*. Times Newspapers Limited: Dilys Powell, review of *Zorba the Greek* (*Sunday Times*, 14 May 1965). Philip Howard, *For liking Yinglish, I should apologise?* (*The Times*). The University of California: Leonard Michaels & Christopher Ricks, *The State of the Language*. John Whitney, former Director General of Independent Broadcasting Authority. Writers and Readers Publishing Cooperative: Arnold Wesker, *Words and Definitions of Experience*.

G.H.

English in the 21st century

English, which began life as a modest dialect brought to England in the 5th century by Germanic tribes, has become the international language of the world. First it was the Norman Conquest in 1066, the one history date everyone remembers, that brought English into the mainstream of European languages, as the vocabulary took on shiploads of words from Norman French. Since then, the language has become ever more versatile and widespread, until now, in the 21st century, it is estimated that six-tenths of the world's radio and television programmes and seven-tenths of all the letters written every day are in English. Almost wherever you go, you hear English – the international language of aviation, computers and pop music and the obligatory language, or at least a smattering of it, of every waiter, taxi-driver and air hostess.

Everywhere English is being stretched in new directions. Never before has the rhythm of change been faster: we wake up every morning to new discoveries, new concepts and fresh demands on language to express what we think and feel. *Spoken* English has become far more influential now and has lubricated the wheels of the written language, leaving it much more easygoing. Unless we are aware of these changes, our English could seem old-fashioned or stilted.

This book gives quick, easy and authoritative guidance on how difficulties over grammar and the use and pronunciation of words are being resolved now. It is the result of many consultations with writers, editors and broadcasters, followed by countless cross-references to the latest dictionaries and books on linguistics. Here are some of the questions it answers: Are *four-letter words* still taboo? Why is Prince Andrew's speech much less 'public school' than his older brother's? How can we avoid sexist words or words that could give offence to ethnic groups? Do we still have to learn about *who* and *whom*?

There are two ways to look at English grammar. There is the way many of us were taught, that there are definite rules, true for all time. Nowadays few linguistic scholars believe that, because while there is order in the way we should construct sentences there is also some flexibility and freedom. This book draws the line between rules of grammar and usage that should be understood and followed at the present time, in order to write and speak good standard English, and outworn rules that were either never valid to begin with or have dropped away, because they belong with pince-nez, wing-collars and high-button boots.

Dictionaries are indispensable and we should be lost without them. But even the best dictionary reflects the opinions of its editors, which is why dictionaries may disagree over the meaning or pronunciation of certain words. Editors' decisions are invaluable as guidance but not always final: there are times when we – not our dictionary – can decide to have the last word.

Sooner or later dictionaries accept as good English what most people say and write. If anyone argues with that, quote what Robert Burchfield (as chief editor of Oxford English Dictionaries) said on the BBC: 'It is the duty of lexicographers to record actual usage as shown by collected examples, not to express moral approval or disapproval of usage.'

And dictionaries, like railway timetables, become out of date. The meanings of words change and affect us in new ways. Elizabeth Barrett Browning wrote this in a letter, when she was on honeymoon in 1846: 'After two months of uninterrupted intercourse he loves me better every day ... and my health improves too.' She would hardly write that now! English is on the move all the time, leaving your dictionary behind. A new word or the new use of a word is not always wrong because it is not in the dictionary.

The status of words changes too. A word considered slang a few years ago may by now have moved up into standard English, suitable for use in formal writing. During the transition period dictionaries often disagree on whether a word has crossed over into standard English and we have to make up our own minds, or better still take note of how good writers and speakers are using it.

There are occasional words and expressions in this book that some dictionaries classify as slang, colloquial or informal. Other dictionaries may treat some of them as standard English and this may be the general view in a few years' time. These words are used here because they seem appropriate to a balanced approach to English in our time. Change makes many people uneasy, which is why they may over-react to any deviation from so-called rules of English they learned at school ten, twenty, thirty or more years ago. Yet they freely use words and grammatical forms their grandparents would have made just as much fuss about.

When we *contact* a garage to have our car *serviced* or to buy a *reconditioned* engine, when we call in a *babysitter*, *finalize* arrangements or *feature* something in a report, we are using English in only a few of thousands of ways, now accepted but angrily rejected not so many years ago. Further back still, Dr Johnson tried to eliminate words, such as *fun*, *clever*, *budge* and *mob*, among others, that we now take for granted.

All changes are not for the better and some useful distinctions of meaning are lost on the way. But the process of change never becomes a free-for-all: the essential structure of the language remains. Linguistic history has shown that English has its own instinctive genius, absorbing or rejecting changes as it goes along, and still remaining all things to all people in their constant need to communicate.

Many of us have strong personal prejudices about English usage and it is easy to upset or antagonize people by using words in a way they dislike, though respected writers, even some professors of English, may take another view. The following symbols in this book are warnings:

*   A stick-in-the-mud may consider this usage wrong but for most writers and speakers it is perfectly good English.
**   Many more people object to this, especially when used in writing. Where it is generally considered incorrect English, this is always made clear. In other examples, opinions differ and which side you take depends upon the circumstances or how independent and innovative you feel over the use of the language.
*** This would shock many people who would regard it as illiterate or, in the case of some words or expressions, offensive and indecent.

There is one additional symbol:

†   Singles out a useful new word, or a less familiar way of
    using an old word; or an interesting word, unfamiliar to
    some people, that is now coming to the fore and worth
    knowing about.

Abbreviations

COD: *Concise Oxford Dictionary*
LD: *Longmans Dictionary of the English Language*

How to use this book

Although the entries are arranged alphabetically, as in a
dictionary, this book is designed to be read all the way
through: language is not just for grammar books but is there
to be used and enjoyed. To prove that, look at Gray Jolliffe's
'linguistic' cartoons! Those cartoons are there not only to
show that language can be fun, but to help you remember
the points in some of the entries.

Reading through the book first will give you up-to-date
insights into how problems of English usage are being
resolved in the 21st century. From then on, you will know
which entry to turn to for help over grammatical problems
or over the use and pronunciation of words that present
difficulties or which are taking on new meanings.

A

a or **an**

When in doubt say it aloud to see if it *sounds* right. *A* before a consonant: *a* business, *a* sale. *An* before a vowel: *an* army, *an* error. Two possible hang-ups: 1. When words begin with 'h'. Usually it's like a consonant. Use *a*: *a* house, *a* has-been. But with four words we don't sound the 'h', so it becomes a vowel-sound: hour, heir, honour, honest. Use *an*: *an* hour, *an* honourable man. But do not say '*an* hotel' unless you want to sound Edwardian because it belongs to the time when some people said 'an 'otel', dropping the 'h' as in French. 2. When words begin with 'u' pronounced 'yoo', it's like a consonant. Use *a*: *a* union, *a* European. With abbreviations, listen to the sound: an MP (pronounced 'empee'), *a* UNESCO meeting. Watch out for the figure 8 which begins with a vowel-sound. Use *an*: *an* £8 million contract.

AA

An abbreviation with various meanings: Advertising Association, Architectural Association, Automobile Association and Alcoholics Anonymous.

abbreviations

It is now old-fashioned and unnecessary to put stops between the letters of most abbreviations: BBC, TUC, MA, MP, USA. Or stops after Mr, Mrs, Ms, Dr, St (St John's Wood, St Mary's Church). Or stops after shortcuts such as: co-op, demo, recap, repro (reproduction). You can now get up at 7 *am*, even when the temperature is only 5°C, go to bed at 11 *pm*, buy a cup of coffee for 50p – all without stops. *The Times* omits stops between initials in people's names, but not everyone has got round to that yet. It's up to you. Also see **UN**

-able or **-ible**

Is it accessible or accessable, responsible or responsable? Unless you know, the only way to be sure is to look it up in a dictionary. Because there are fewer *-ible* words it's worth learning the more common ones: accessible, admissible, audible, collapsible, compatible, comprehensible, contemptible, credible, defensible, destructible, edible, eligible, fallible, feasible, flexible, forcible, gullible, indelible, intelligible, legible, negligible, perceptible, permissible, plausible, possible, responsible, reversible, sensible, susceptible, tangible, visible.

Until writing was invented, man lived in acoustic space: boundless, directionless, horizonless, in the dark of the mind, in the world of emotion, by primordial intuition, by terror. Speech is a social chart of this bog.
Marshall McLuhan, *The Medium is the Massage*

abnormal or subnormal
People sometimes mix them up. *Abnormal*: anything different from normal; *subnormal*: anything below normal. When they are used about people, both words have a bad sense now so it can sound gentler to use *not normal* or *below normal*. *Above normal* is also possible, of course, but if something or someone is out of this world, use *supernormal*.

academic
We no longer believe that intellectual concepts can solve the world's problems. Too often they have gone badly wrong. So now if we say 'his approach is academic' we usually mean it is up in the clouds and irrelevant. An *academic question* is of no real importance. When an art critic says a painting is *academic*, he would mean now that it is formal, conventional and dull. If you use *academic* in the old Platonic sense of scholarly and wise, you will probably be misunderstood.

accents
The accent of the British 'upper class' used to be called a 'public school accent' and was considered to be a great asset. All that has changed and the 'I say old chap!' voice can now sound affected and out of touch. Many successful people, from cabinet ministers to professors, speak with an 'ordinary' accent. So do most of the young trendsetters. Prince Andrew's speech, for example, is much less 'public school' than his older brother's. Ted Hughes, as Poet Laureate, intoned his poetry in a strong Yorkshire accent, and regional accents are part of the appeal of Michael Caine, Julie Walters and others. Except for a few die-hards, our whole idea of what it means to 'talk prop-

er' has been turned upside down. And that's good news. See **class language**

Twenty years ago, the bright young of working-class origin with intellectual gifts or talents would have been likely to acquire a BBC accent and pass as upper middle-class. Today they feel no need to hide their accent. They are the new trend-setters.

Geoffrey Gorer, *Sex and Marriage in England Today*

accommodate

Many people spell it wrongly and many more are eager to point it out. Always *double c – double m.*

acknowledgement or **acknowledgment**

Either but *acknowledgement* is preferred. Compare abridgement, amazement. When *-ment* is added to a word ending in a silent *-e*, the *-e* usually stays.

acoustics

When it's a science, always singular: '*Acoustics* is an interesting subject.' When it's the qualities in a hall, always plural: 'The *acoustics* of the Royal Festival Hall *are* very good.' Remember, only *one c.*

actually

If you say 'We're going to get married actually', the word *actually* is meaningless social affectation. But you can use *actually* to give a sentence a real 'how about that?' flavour: 'We're *actually* going to get married!'

ad or **advert**

Almost everyone in advertising talks about 'a great ad' (and you don't need a stop after it), but never about 'a great advert'. *Ad* is all right (at least in conversation) but *advert* is downmarket.

adapter or **adaptor**

Although these words are now considered interchange-able, they are still often used to denote different things: an *adapter* is a *person*, someone who adapts, say a book for television or a piece of equipment to serve another purpose. An *adaptor* is an *object*, commonly an electrical fitting used to adapt one kind of plug to another kind of socket.

adman†

In Madison Avenue, centre of New York's advertising business, they have talked about *admen* for many years. One Oxford dictionary even seems to accept it now as standard English; most copywriters and executives in British ad agencies are happy to be called *admen*. *Ad agency* – two words; *adman* – one word. Neither is hyphenated.

adverse or **averse**

It is easy to see how even good writers occasionally mix up these two words. If you are *adverse* to something you are against it, its *adversary*: 'I am *adverse* to you getting married.' If you are *averse* to something, you have a strong distaste for it, an *aversion* for it. But there's no need for such a pompous expression as 'I'm not averse to a whisky.' If you want a drink, why not say so? Pronunciation: 'ADverse' and 'aVERSE'.

advert or **ad**

See **ad**

aerobic†

Many joggers who use this word freely are unaware that it is a biological term, derived from Greek words meaning air and life, used for describing a microbe living off oxygen from the air. These days fitness experts use *aerobic* in another way, which surprisingly is not explained in some dictionaries. *Aerobic* describes steady (rather than violent) exercise, that must be sustained long enough to induce a prescribed rate of heartbeat and respiration. The exercises are called *aerobics*. Pronounce it: 'airROBEics'. See **jogging**

aerodrome

This word is still in dictionaries but if you use it you will sound like a World War I pilot. The words now are: **airfield** or *airport* (an important *airfield* with facilities for passengers and customs).

aeroplane or **airplane** or **aircraft**

It depends upon whether you are British, American or in the RAF. You fly from Heathrow, London's airport, in an *aeroplane*. You take off from Kennedy Airport, New York in an *airplane*. The RAF fly *aircraft*, a useful word because it is both singular and plural ('a squadron of twelve aircraft') and also includes helicopters, which *aeroplane* and *airplane* do not.

aerospace†

This is a word that we shall hear more and more because it includes both the earth's atmosphere and also outer space. So a journey in *aerospace* could cover a quick hop over to Paris or a voyage to the moon.

affect or effect

Affect means to have an influence on something or somebody in an unexplained way: 'She was much *affected* by what he said.' But you don't know *how* she was affected so why not say what you mean: 'She was much encouraged by what he said.' *Effect* means to make something happen: 'The bonus scheme *effected* a big increase in productivity.'

Afghanistan

This is the country that saw the first war of the 21st century. The people are called *Afghans*. Some dictionaries show *Afghanis* as an alternative, but it is as misguided to use that name as it would be to call a tall graceful Afghan hound an *Afghani*. You may hear *Afghan* for the language, but the preferred official name is *Pashto*. The *Pashtuns* are the people who speak that language, and this is preferable to *Pathans*, the academic Hindi name. The other main language is *Dari* (pron: 'DAHry'), the name used in Afghanistan for modern Persian (called *Farsi* in Iran). The pronunciation of the capital, Kabul, hovers between 'KAHbool' and 'kerBOOL', both of which are heard.

aged

Remember there are two meanings and it depends upon how you say it. As *two* syllables (pron: 'AY-jid') it means someone is very old. As *one* syllable (pron: 'ayjd') it is simply a way of saying someone's age: 'She is *aged* seven.' *Aged* is also *one* syllable when 'Whisky is *aged* in casks', or 'He has *aged* greatly since her death.'

agenda

Some Latin scholars still prefer *agendum* for the singular and *agenda* for plural; and if you were living in Ancient Rome that would be spot-on. But nowadays nearly everyone says or writes *agenda* for one and *agendas* for more than one.

aggravate

From the Latin *aggravare* meaning 'to make heavy' (think

of gravity). It means making a bad situation worse: 'His
illness was *aggravated* by overwork.' It is also commonly
used as a way of saying to annoy or upset someone: 'My
children *aggravate* me so much.'** Many people still consider the latter uneducated even though it has been used
that way for over 200 years.

aircraft

See **aeroplane**

airfield

See **aerodrome**

airplane

See **aeroplane**

all alone

Fusspots criticize this, saying that *all* is unnecessary, since
you are either alone or not alone. Using language is more
subtle than working a machine efficiently and if you want
to stress how lonely or frightened you are, *all alone* is a
good way of putting it. For some people 'lonesome' is a
cosier word, and although it is sometimes attacked as an
Americanism, it has been used in English since the 17th
century. If you feel lonesome, go ahead and say so.

> *Alone, alone, all, all alone,*
> *Alone on a wide, wide sea*!
> Samuel Coleridge, *The Ancient Mariner*

allergic and **allergy**

These began as strictly medical terms describing hyper-
sensitivity to anything. If eggs make you ill or roses make
you sneeze, you are *allergic* to them. The words came to
be used loosely for almost anything you dislike intensely:
'Margaret Thatcher is *allergic* to changing her mind.'
Nowadays we understand more and more that reactions
to different foods can cause many physical and psychological problems and the medical applications of *allergic*
and *allergy* are much more important. It is preferable to
use these words now only about things that make you ill
in one way or another.

all right or **alright**

Although you see *alright*** sometimes, even in *The Times*,
it still seems an uneducated form of *all right*. Better not

use it unless you want to make a fight for it because of 'already', 'almost', 'almighty', etc.

all together or **altogether**

They mean different things. *All together* is when a number of things are happening or a number of people are somewhere *at the same time*: 'The women arrived *all together*.' '*All together* now – let's sing!' *Altogether* means totally, with nothing left out: 'He has had three wives *altogether*.' (If he had three wives all together, he would have had them all at the same time.) To be 'in the altogether' is something else *altogether*. It is a prissy way of saying you are naked.

alright

See **all right**

alternative

'We are considering several *alternatives*.' Some older people argue that, because of the Latin derivation of the word, *alternative* can be used only for a choice between two things. That's as old-fashioned as bowler hats, and recent dictionaries state that *alternative* now means a choice between two *or more* things.

I wouldn't have chosen an alternative lifestyle had there been any alternative.

The word *alternative* has also been used for some time now to describe an off-beat life-style, breaking away from established conventions of society. People in communes call themselves the *alternative society*.

although or **though**

It does not matter which one you use, except when you say or write *even though*.

altogether

See **all together**

aluminium or **aluminum**

Aluminium in Britain (pron: 'aluMINyum'). *Aluminum* in the US (pron: 'aLOOminum').

ambiance or **ambience**

The French word is *ambiance* which is regarded as a foreign word used in English. The English word is *ambience*. You can use either. It's a useful word because it covers not only the general surroundings of a place but the atmosphere as well: 'The restaurant has a warm friendly ambience.' Pronounce *ambiance* more or less the French way: 'AMbeeahns' and *ambience* as in English.

amend or **emend**

Nearly always the word you want is *amend*, whether it is to make an improvement in something or to correct errors in something that has been written ('She *amended* the draft of the letter'). *Emend* has a much more limited meaning, covering changes (not necessarily corrections) in a text: 'The draft agreement was *emended* to cover the new conditions.'

Americanisms

Some people get very steamed up when American expressions are used in Britain. The magistral H.W. Fowler proclaimed: 'Americanisms are foreign words and should be so treated.' Take that to heart and we throw out teenager, babysitter, crank, bluff, boom, slump, stunt, paperback, room-mate and hundreds of other words that we should be lost without. We share so much with the US through the cinema, television and technology that it would be artificial to force the two versions of English apart. British English has its own way of rejecting many Americanisms it does not like, such as the American spelling of -our as -or in words such as 'color', 'honor', 'favor', 'glamor'. We have chosen also to reject some useful American words, such as 'sidewalk'.

Both versions of the English language have their own genius and if an American expression comes naturally to you, there is no need to lose any sleep over using it. Either the rest of us will also use it sooner or later, or it will never catch on and you will get the message.

What would English writing, left to the English, by now have become? To try to imagine it without immigrant influences, as well as without American influences, bouncing back at it in ceaseless bombardment, is to think of something hushed and secret: a club for initiates, housing a subtle and exclusive language of gesture, understatement, unstatement.

Times Literary Supplement

among or **amongst**
Older people or literary people may still use *amongst*. It is interchangeable with *among*, so unless you happen to enjoy the sound of *amongst*, you can forget about it.

amoral or **immoral**
The difference between these words is important. An *amoral* person does not recognize or acknowledge morals or the concept of 'right' and 'wrong'. Dr Margaret Wright, the psychiatrist, says that this is a psychopathic state. It can also be a philosophical attitude. To be *immoral* you have to *do* something that society considers evil, dissolute or depraved. The problem with *immorality* is that morals are not absolute and can vary from one society to another. In sexual relationships, there are people who believe that even minor deviations are *immoral*. At the same time, the sexologist Dr Alex Comfort advises that 'the whole joy of sex-with-love is that there are no rules, so long as you enjoy, and the choice is practically unlimited'. In the 21st century, *immoral* is a word to use with caution.
Amoral – one *m*; *immoral* – two *m*s.

and
Here is one of the simplest and oldest words in English yet people can still hesitate over how to use it. The trouble is that some schools teach that you should never begin a sentence with the word *and*. That has always been nonsense: look at the first dozen or so sentences of the Authorized

Version of the Bible, published in 1611 and translated by forty-seven of the leading scholars at the time. Most of those sentences begin with *And*. Or look at the 1984 *LD*: 'There are many occasions on which it is perfectly legitimate and very effective to begin a sentence with *and*.'

angst†

It is not surprising that this German word, which took up residence in England years ago, is more and more in demand these days, since it describes a general feeling of anxiety about anything, but especially about the state of the world and the human condition. To experience *angst* (pronounce it exactly as it is spelt) look at the news on TV almost any evening or open any newspaper.

anorexia†

Short for *anorexia nervosa* (pron: 'annaREXia nerVOHsa'). Although described in medical writings over 100 years ago, this has become a disorder of *our* time, the grotesque condition of starving in the midst of plenty. Advertising makes us believe that 'thin is beautiful', 'fat is ugly', and some young women (rarely men) become terrified of eating, almost to the point of death from starvation. These victims of the pressures of society have, according to the psychiatrist Edward Stonehill, an abnormal fear of growing up.

ante- or **anti-**

Ante- comes from Latin and means 'before'. When you

put up an ante in poker, you put down your stake before drawing cards. Think of *antenatal* clinics. *Anti-* is from Greek and means 'against' or 'opposite': antidote, anticlimax, anticlockwise, antiseptic, antisocial and many other words. Both are pronounced the same: 'anty' (to rhyme with 'shanty'). For anti-, Americans usually say 'ant-eye'.

antediluvian†

You are not likely to want to describe the period before the Flood, Noah's Ark and all that, which is, of course, what this word really means. But it is also an emphatic way of saying that something is altogether out-of-date or utterly old hat. But now that technology and ideas are changing so rapidly, even yesterday's way of doing something could be – *antediluvian*. Pron: 'anteediLUvian'.

anti- or **ante-**

See **ante-**

anti-hero†

The classic idea of a hero is a man (although *hero* is now sometimes used also for a woman) with noble qualities, courage and unselfishness. Heroes were admirable but they could also be boring. So we now have the *anti-hero*, more likely to come home drunk than kneel at a woman's feet. Perhaps it all started in the late 1950s with Jimmy Porter in John Osborne's play *Look Back in Anger*. Many actors, from Jeremy Irons to Gérard Depardieu, play more *anti-heroes* than heroes. See also **heroine**

antisocial†

This is not a new word, since it was used in the 18th century. Its original meaning, defined by the *Shorter Oxford Dictionary* as 'opposed to the principles on which society is constituted', has become blurred and it is now used loosely to describe almost any behaviour that doesn't suit someone at that moment. So if you refuse a drink or you smoke a cigarette in the wrong place, you might well be accused of being *antisocial*. *Antisocial* is one word now and there is no need for a hyphen.

anyone or **any one**

It doesn't matter much although it's better to keep it as one word unless it is one of a number, when it looks better as two words: 'You can do it in *any one* of six different ways.' See **everybody**

any place

The usual English word is 'anywhere' but there's nothing wrong with *any place* ('I can't find it *any* place') if you don't mind sounding slightly American.

anyway or **any way**

One word, although in 'You can do it *any way* you like', some people prefer *two* words. Anyway there are more important things to think about.

apartheid

This word, and all the human misery it encompasses, is often in the news. It is used sometimes for segregation of any kind, but since it first arose from racial segregation in South Africa, it is safer to use it only in that context. As it is Afrikaans, it is not easy to know how to pronounce it. You hear 'apartite' and Senator Edward Kennedy used to say 'apart-hide'. The approved pronunciation is: 'aPAHThate' which makes the sound of the word like the meaning of it.

apartment

The American word for 'flat' has become quite common in London now and is used by some estate agents, especially for grand and expensive flats. But don't use it if you live in a modest bed-sitter.

appendix

The Latinate plural *appendices* is beginning to sound affected. It is, of course, not 'wrong' but most people now are more at home saying and writing *appendixes*.

I am the Roman Emperor, and am above grammar.
                                        Emperor Sigismund I (1361-1437)

applicable

Because of *apply* (pron: 'apPLY'), many people find it easier to say apPLICable* which is now an acceptable pronunciation (*COD* and *LD*). But the upmarket pronunciation is 'APplicable', with the stress on the *first* syllable.

arbitrarily

The approved pronunciation is 'ARbitrarily' (with only the *first* syllable stressed), which is not so easy to say. For that reason, 'arbiTRARily' is often heard and is generally accepted.*

aristocrat

If you want to sound like one you will put the stress on the *first* syllable: 'ARistocrat'. Otherwise you can say 'aRIStocrat'** given as an alternative in *LD*.

around or **round**

'The wheels go *round*' but we can look '*around* the corner' or *round* it. London Transport issued a book called 'Country Walks *Around* London'. As you can see, it's something of a free-for-all, so you can say whatever comes naturally. Most of us are happy saying 'Come for a drink *around* seven o'clock', or 'There were *around* 30 people in the room.' Others complain that this is an Americanism and that we must say 'about seven o'clock', 'about 30 people'. Nevertheless, this use of *around* for 'about' has crossed the Atlantic and has settled down comfortably here.

It was American English that carried the language to the furthest corners of the globe. Blue jeans and Hollywood movies played their part in this, but it was Cruise missiles and Stealth bombers that became crucial to the process.

Robert McCrum in the *Observer*

arse**

Most dictionaries say it is rude. But listen to Eric Partridge, who was one of the foremost experts on English: '*Arse*, an excellent old English word, is no longer obscene.' So you have to decide for yourself whether you sit on your bottom, behind, buttocks or your *arse*. Americans spell and pronounce the word 'ass' and use it without any connotation of obscenity at all. No one seems to mind 'bum'* although it is beginning to sound rather coy. *Arsehole****, in some company, will produce a shocked silence, although, if you're lucky, you may get away with *arselicker***, not infrequently used to describe someone who will do anything to please the boss.

Asian or **Asiatic**

Asiatic is now a racist word and we should describe people from India, China, Japan and all the other countries in what is the world's largest continent as *Asian*. This makes *Asian* the direct parallel to 'European'. It is all right to use *Asiatic* in scientific or geographical contexts such as 'The Royal *Asiatic* Society'. See **racist words**

assurance or insurance

Insurance companies continue to issue *insurance* policies for your car, house, holidays and so on but *assurance* policies for your life. It is an old-fashioned and unnecessary confusion for the rest of us but there it is. *Assurance*, in this sense, is no longer used in the US and it is time it was dropped here.

assure or ensure or insure

Your insurance broker might say: 'I *assure* you that I have *ensured* that you are fully *insured*.' *Assure* is used from one person to another to mean 'promise' or 'guarantee'. *Ensure* means 'to make certain'. Finally, *insure* is restricted to financial protection through insurance. Read the first sentence again and it should all become clear. In the US, *insure* is also used the way we use ensure, to mean 'to make certain', but that would be a confusing use in Britain.

astronaut or cosmonaut†

The US calls travellers in outer space *astronauts*. *Cosmonauts* (partly adapted from the Russian word) is used for Soviet *astronauts*.

ate

In the US they make it rhyme with 'fate'. In Britain it rhymes with 'bet'.

at the end of the day and at this moment in time

It has become fashionable to criticize *at this moment in time* as a long-winded way of saying 'now' or 'at present'. Some good writers have told me that they like to use it occasionally because it has a certain cosmic ring to it. So use it when it suits you but not so often that it becomes boring. The same applies to *at the end of the day* which, in the right place, has a biblical flavour.

avant-garde†

In French it is still used as a military term for a guard sent out in advance but in 19th-century France it also became a literary and artistic expression for experimenters who led new movements in the arts. It is used that way as a fully naturalized English word: 'the *avant-garde* theatre', 'an *avant-garde* novel'. But it is now being used more and more for any breakaway from the accepted way of doing things. When the writer, Rose Macaulay, urged a priest to go in for a 'Jazz Mass', she said he ought to be *'avant-garde* from time to time'. Whether you are a drop-out or simply *avant-garde* depends upon how someone else looks at it. Pronounce it the French way: 'avahn-gahd'.

averse or **adverse**

See **adverse**

awake

This ordinary word causes so much confusion that we can sympathize with Irving Berlin's song 'Oh how I hate to get up in the morning!' Were you *awakened* by the alarm clock, *awoken* by it, or *woken up*? If you want to keep the grammarians happy, you will be *awakened* by it. That is 'right' but so few people make the distinction that you are unlikely to be criticized if you use the other versions.

When I started in 1982, every newspaper article you read told us that the book was dead. But don't tell Waterstone's now that the book is dead or dying! Simple, collectable, giveable, beautiful thing that it is, it never will die.

Tim Waterstone in the *Financial Times*

B

babysitter

This indispensable importation from the US has become as common as 'teapot' and like that word, there is no need to hyphenate it any more ('baby-sitter'), although it still appears that way in some dictionaries.

backlog

A useful word, borrowed from the US where its literal meaning is a large log put at the back of the fireplace to keep the fire going. It still has the meaning there of something in reserve, so an American businessman is happy to have a *backlog* of orders. In Britain, *backlog* has taken on a negative meaning, usually implying a pile up of work due to strikes or other problems. In America, you look cheerful about a *backlog*; in Britain, you have a long face.

balance of trade†

On the lips of every chancellor of the exchequer, although not everyone knows what it means, even though a writer was using it as far back as the 17th century. *Balance of trade* is the difference in value between what we export and what we import.

'What if a critic construes a poem in a way you felt you didn't mean?'
'I should think he was talking balls.'
  Philip Larkin, *Poets in Conversation with John Haffenden*

balls**

I have never heard even the most formal of men say 'My testicles ache.' It is always 'My *balls* ache.' Yet most dictionaries still classify the word as 'vulgar'. As for that vivid expression, *balls-up*, meaning a complete mess of something, it is freely used by so many people, including David Watt, as Director of the Royal Institute of International Affairs, who once said: 'Harold Nicolson and Lord Robert Cecil felt that the great men were making a fearful *balls-up*, as indeed they were.' Surely after that, if someone makes a *balls-up*, you can say so in almost any company. *Balls**, meaning a load of nonsense, is safe enough unless you want to be especially careful. See **cock**

balmy or **barmy**

Apart from their literal meanings (balm – something that is soothing; barm – the froth of fermenting yeast), these friendly words have been in use interchangeably since the 17th century to mean slightly mad or daft. The most literate people use them that way, even in writing sometimes, so it seems *barmy* that some dictionaries, although not all, still regard them as 'slang'.

barbaric or **barbarous**

Barbaric means crude and uncivilized in style or manner. To the Romans any non-Roman was *barbaric*. *Barbarous* is often used to mean the same as *barbaric* but it is in fact a much more severe word, stressing cruelty and harshness of actions or behaviour: 'He treated her *barbarously*.'

bastard

A woman who chooses the experience of motherhood but rejects the convention of marriage would rightly turn on you if you called her child a *bastard*. A few years ago statistics were released in the UK telling us that 'One in five babies is born to a single-parent mother.' The old stigma of illegitimacy is fading and the words *bastard* and *illegitimate*, to describe a child born outside legal marriage, are outmoded, belonging as they do to a system of social values that some people no longer accept. *Bastard* is also used, mostly by women, as an emotive description for a man, who is, to say the least, unpopular.

BBC or the Beeb

Those who work for the BBC sometimes show they are 'in the know' by calling it the *Beeb*. It is like the way some people referred to Lord Olivier as 'Larry', implying an intimacy that might or might not have been true.

behove

If you don't mind talking like a character out of a Victorian novel, you can still use this word but it must *always* be preceded by 'it': 'It *behoves* you to take care how you speak to me.' I prefer 'You should be careful what you say to me.' Americans spell it *behoove* and pronounce it that way.

belly

Although some people think they are too refined to use this word because they think it is slightly rude, *no* dictionary classifies it as 'vulgar'. It is a good down-to-earth old English word, so no one need hesitate to say they have a *bellyache* or have had a *bellyful* of anything or anybody.

Words are best and old words best of all.

Winston Churchill

beloved

Pronounced two ways. In 'my *beloved* husband', the -ed is a separate syllable, even if it does sound a little poetic: 'belov-ed'. In 'she is *beloved* by all', pronounce it 'belov'd'.

bent

Be wary of this word because in its *slang* usage it has two meanings. The older meaning is to be corrupt or dishonest. The second meaning, ignored by most dictionaries although it has existed for some years now, is to be homosexual. The second usage is so widespread that it is beginning to take over from the earlier slang meaning and there is a risk of an awkward misunderstanding. The opposite of *bent*, *straight*, is the slang word occasionally used by homosexuals when referring to heterosexuals.

Berkeley

If you are listening to the nightingales in *Berkeley* Square in London, pronounce it 'Barkley'. If you are a student at the fashionable *Berkeley* University in California, the first syllable rhymes with 'Ber' in Berlin: 'Berkley'.

between

Some older people and older dictionaries say that *between* relates only to *two* persons or things and that when there are more than two, 'among' must be used. That is an old-fashioned idea and recent dictionaries allow *between* to refer to any number: 'Let's divide the bill *between* all six of us.' See **alternative**

between you and I*

See **I**

bi-

Biannual means twice a year and there's no problem there. But *bimonthly* and *biweekly* are now taken to mean *either* every two months, every two weeks *or* twice a month, twice a week. So it is better to say exactly what you mean: 'every two weeks', 'twice a month', and so on. And ask what someone else means if it is not clear. There is no problem over *bilateral* which always means two-sided: 'It was a *bilateral* decision.'

bikini

This is the only happy by-product of nuclear experiments. *Bikini* is the name of the atoll in the Pacific where the US staged an atomic explosion in 1946. A clever designer fastened on to the name to suggest the explosive effect on a man of a woman wearing such a minimal swimsuit and *bikini* crossed nearly every frontier to become an international word. When topless bathing for women became more frequent, *monokini* was tried but never caught on, so in the end we are left with *bikini bottom*.

billboard†

A *billboard* in America is the same as a 'hoarding' (for outdoor advertising) in England. Of the two, *billboard* is the better word because it is more descriptive and some people in England now use it, although it is not generally accepted. Use *billboard* if you prefer it.

> *I think that I shall never see*
> *A billboard lovely as a tree.*
> *Indeed, unless the billboards fall,*
> *I'll never see a tree at all!*
>
>   Ogden Nash, *Song of the Open Road*

billion

Formerly always a million million in Europe, but a thousand million in America. The American definition has taken over so nearly always now people will assume you mean a thousand million unless you say otherwise.

black or coloured

Coloured, used for people who are not white, is associated with **apartheid**, and *black* (usually without a capital) should be used for people of African or Afro-Caribbean origin. Black goes beyond skin colour to identify common cultural and life experiences of black people. In the USA, the compound African-American is increasingly preferred. See **Asian** and **racist words**

bloke

Nowadays a woman is more likely to say she is going out with a 'feller' or a 'man' rather than with a *bloke*. *Bloke* was a low-class word until about 1900 and then later on it became fashionable. But it has a dusty unused look about it now. See **boyfriend**

blond or blonde

The title of an old Marilyn Monroe film was *Gentlemen Prefer Blondes* (with an *-e*). Women have *blonde* hair (also with an *-e*). But if a man is fair, he has *blond* hair.

bloody*

On 11 April 1914, Mrs Patrick Campbell, playing Eliza Doolittle in Bernard Shaw's *Pygmalion*, caused a sensation at the first night with the line 'Walk! Not *bloody* likely. I am going in a taxi.' In the years since then, *bloody* has become almost as inoffensive as 'dear me'. I have heard a bishop say 'It's a *bloody* awful situation.' As for *bloody-minded*, meaning deliberately obstructive and unhelpful, nearly everyone uses it anywhere and the *LD* now treats it as standard English.

blouse

For some time, unisex has been forcing a common name

for both women's and men's clothes and feminists do not seem to object to the names of men's clothes taking over. *Blouse* now sounds fuddy-duddy and most younger women wear 'shirts', although for something frilly and fancy, the word *blouse* is taken out, dusted and re-used.

blow up or **blow-up**

You *blow up* (no hyphen) a picture and the result is a *blow-up* (with a hyphen).

blue

Blue has been used in standard English for a long time to mean melancholy (like the *blues* in black American jazz). Another meaning, which goes back to the 19th century (although for some reason it is not given in some dictionaries), is pornographic or obscene and one still hears and reads this usage occasionally: '*blue* movies', '*blue* language'. See **pornography**

blueprint

This word from engineering terminology is freely used now, some say too freely, to describe a plan for any project: 'The *blueprint* for a successful sales campaign.' But we should use it to mean a final detailed programme, not an outline scheme, because in engineering a *blueprint* marks the final stage of the design on the drawing-board.

blurb

Because it seems a funny word, many people think that *blurb* is slang. Every dictionary now classifies it as standard English and it is used in the most august literary circles to describe a publisher's sales description of a book. The *blurb* for *A Guide to English in the 21st Century* is on the inside flap of the jacket. By extension, *blurb* is now also used for any short sales pitch in speech or writing. The word was invented in the 1920s by an American humorist, Gelett Burgess, and passed effortlessly into standard language on both sides of the Atlantic.

board

Do we say 'The board *has* decided' or '*have* decided'? Either will do in most cases but you cannot have it both ways and write 'The board *has* not yet given *their* decision.' If you use 'has', it has to be followed by 'its decision'. When you're talking about the individual members, it is more natural to treat the word as plural: 'The *board* are now having lunch', 'The *board* are unable to make up their minds.'

boat or ship

Sailors usually know which word to use but landlubbers are sometimes afraid of making a gaffe. Strictly speaking, a *boat* is a small *ship*. But a fishing trawler, no matter how big, is always 'a fishing boat'. When cargo or passengers are carried it is usually in a *ship*. But passengers on cross-Channel ferries, some of which are now large and comfortable, sail on a cross-Channel *boat*. A millionaire's yacht, with all its spacious luxury, remains a sailing *boat*, yet 'I spied three *ships* come sailing by'. In the Royal Navy, almost anything afloat is HMS – Her Majesty's *Ship*, unless it is a *boat* launched from a *ship*. A flying *ship* would be a fantasy but a flying *boat* exists. And even in the smallest *boat*, everything should be ship-shape. I hope these notes will help you to steer the right course and if in doubt, you can always fall back on the word 'vessel', which is what dictionaries do sometimes.

Dictionaries are like watches; the worst is better than none, and the best cannot be expected to go quite true.
  Samuel Johnson, *Anecdotes of the late Samuel Johnson*

bon appétit

When a French friend of mine raised his glass at dinner and said 'Good appetite!', everyone looked startled. This familiar French phrase is untranslatable into English. So if those are your sentiments, then you'd better say it in French – *Bon appétit*!

boobs

This word, from London in the 1960s, is the word most women in the UK use for breasts. Men use it as well and although dictionaries classify *boobs* as slang, none of them lists it as vulgar. As a result, 'breasts' has become rather formal although it remains the clinical term. A *boob* has also come to mean a blunder or faux-pas.

boss

The *COD* treats it as 'colloq.' but the *LD* rightly includes it as standard English since it is now used in serious discussions by BBC newscasters and in Parliament. In the US it has a negative aspect, especially when used for the *boss* of a union or of a political organization. As a verb, 'to *boss* someone about', it is still considered informal and it is better to use it that way only in conversation or in casual writing.

both

It should still be used about only *two* things or people and it is wrong to say '*Both* John, Mary and Helen are coming to dinner.' If you want to emphasize more than two, simply say 'all three of them', etc. Some people criticize the use of *both* for 'each', claiming that 'There is a chemist on *both* sides of the street' means that the chemist straddles the street. But the use of *both* in this way is common and the meaning is completely clear, at least in the above example.

boyfriend

In the past when a couple lived together without getting married, a shocked or discreet silence prevailed. But now this is so common that we need a word for the relationship. Some women make a distinction between 'a' *boyfriend* and 'my' *boyfriend*, the latter meaning the man she goes to bed with. Some of us find this coy and evasive and Philip Howard, when literary editor of *The Times*, devoted a chapter in his book, *Words Fail Me*, to other solutions to this linguistic problem. He tells us that the Social Services Correspondent of *The Times* tried 'cohabitee' but no one liked it. He quotes Section 34 of the Supplementary Benefits Act 1976 which defines an unmarried couple as 'living together as husband and wife otherwise than in prescribed circumstances', and suggests this as a helpful introduction at dinner parties: 'Hello, this is Isabel (or Reginald), my current *Section 34*.'

Following up variants in the US, Philip Howard found that the Ford Foundation favours 'meaningful associate' ('Hello Dad! Meet my meaningful associate') and that some American maternity hospitals advise women that they may have present at delivery 'a designated significant other person'. In New York, I have heard a woman quite seriously introduce a man as 'my significant other'. You also hear 'apartmate' in the US, but this implies someone sharing your flat, not necessarily your bed.

Quite an engaging short story has been published in the States about a man and a woman who decide to get married after three years of living together, because they can find no suitable word to describe their relationship when introducing each other: 'And so they were wed, victims of a failure in language.'

Philip Howard, *Words Fail Me*

In pre-feminist days, it was common for some men to introduce their woman as 'my bird' but that sounds old-fashioned cockney slang now. 'My lady' is currently used in London and does have a nice chivalrous ring to it; but, as Philip Howard comments, the opposite, 'my man', sounds like 'Me Jane – you Tarzan'. *Boyfriend* and *girlfriend* remain the words often used regardless of age – witness a newspaper headline: BOYFRIEND, 92, STABS GIRLFRIEND, 84! But another word has now become statutory. *Partner* is used on official forms for the woman or man of a cohabiting couple.

I hope the above notes are of some help in this complicated linguistic headache of our time.

bra

At least one dictionary still states solemnly that this is 'a slang abbreviation of brassière'. The truth is that only a very sedate dowager duchess would ever dream now of calling a 'brassière' anything else but – a *bra*, which has been standard English for years.

brainwashing

We should never forget this word, first heard in the early 1950s as an imitation of the Chinese phrase describing psychological techniques practised in China on political prisoners and prisoners of war, whereby mental attitudes were completely reshaped. In the West, we need to be on guard against *brainwashing*, admittedly of a less sinister nature, in television commercials and political TV programmes. See **psycholinguistics**

breakdown

The two meanings can cause confusion. The first meaning is a total failure to function or to make progress: 'a nervous breakdown', 'a *breakdown* of negotiations', 'a marriage breakdown'. The other meaning is to analyse or divide up into categories: 'a *breakdown* of sales region by region'. But someone could get the wrong idea from: 'a *breakdown* of the business' or 'a *breakdown* of hospital patients by sex'. In those examples 'analysis' and 'classification' would be better. Always think twice when you use *breakdown* in this way.

breasts

See **boobs**

breath or **breathe**

Take a deep *breath* and then *breathe* out. Remember that sentence and you will always use these words in the right way.

bugger**

Dictionaries do not classify *bugger* (in its literal meaning) as 'vulgar', yet it would disgust some people, either because they are not quite sure what it means or because anal intercourse is a taboo. *Bugger* is a vicious term of abuse, yet strangely enough, it is also used in a warm friendly way, even with a hint of admiration: 'You old *bugger*!' It all depends upon how you say it! *Bugger-all** as in 'There's bugger-all to do here' is slang, of course, but not generally regarded as offensive. Dylan Thomas called his first version of *Under Milk Wood 'Llareggub'* (*buggerall* backwards!).

bum*

See **arse****. The US use of *bum* to mean a layabout or good-for-nothing has also caught on in the UK.

but

Contrary to what is still often taught, the official guide for civil servants on the use of English states positively *'But ...* may be freely used to begin either a sentence or a paragraph.' And why not? See **and**

butch

Sometimes it is altogether unpredictable whether a word is 'slang' or has become standard English. Who would have thought that two reputable dictionaries classify *butch*, for a mannish-looking lesbian, as good respectable English used in serious writing? *Baby butch* is used in the US for a young boyish-looking woman.

Byzantine

Thanks to package holidays in Greece, Cyprus and Turkey, *Byzantine* is now sprinkled liberally in travel brochures and guidebooks. This very old rich word, from the ancient Greek city of Byzantium (now Istanbul), founded in the 7th century BC on the shores of the Bosporus, is used in almost as many different ways as it is pronounced. Unless you want to study it in depth, it is safer to use *Byzantine* above all for religious art, the architecture of churches that makes special use of the round arch, the dome dominating a cross with the four aisles of equal length, and for lavish stylized mosaics. The great period was the 4th, 5th and 6th centuries, and perhaps the most renowned example is Sta Sophia in Istanbul. Because the politics of Byzantium were complicated, *Byzantine* has become used also to describe something obscure or devious (as you would expect, it came in for a lot of use during Richard Nixon's presidency). The 'in' pronunciation, favoured by classical scholars, is 'BIZZantyne' (stress on first syllable) but 'byeZANtyne' or 'bizzANtyne' (stress on second syllable) is generally recommended.

C

cad

An Oxford dictionary, as recent as the 1990s, defines *cad* as a 'man who behaves dishonourably'. But does anyone call anyone a *cad* any more?

calendar or **calender** or **colander**

Pirelli Tyres were famous for their *calendars* (now collectors' pieces) with fabulous photographs of beautiful women, and which in passing also showed the date, because that's what a *calendar* is really for. A *calender* is a machine used in processing paper and a *colander* is used in the kitchen to strain vegetables.

calorie

Many people count *calories* but few know what the word means. It is a term from physics now used mainly to describe the energy-producing value of different foods. One *calorie* is the amount of energy required to raise the temperature of 1 gram of water by 1°C. Will that help next time you eat a cream cake?

camp

Used much more about homosexuals before the word 'gay' took over in the 1960s. *Camp* is still used as slang in the UK and the US for outrageously theatrical behaviour ('a marvellous piece of high camp'). In this way, it does not necessarily imply homosexuality; it was, after all, theatrical jargon to begin with, as far back as the 16th century.

can or **may**

Can means it is possible ('I can do it for you because I know how to'); *may* means it is permissible ('I *may* do it for you because I have permission to'). But this distinction, even among good writers, has all but disappeared and can is now frequently used in both senses: 'You *can* go home now.' It is still worth trying to preserve the useful difference of meaning.

cannabis

'Pot', 'dope' or 'grass' are the popular names for marijuana which is a milder form of *cannabis* (produced from the dried leaves of hemp), correctly spelt with *two n*s and not with a capital 'C' unless referring to the botanical species.

can't
See **contracted forms**

capitalist
Not so long ago it was all right to call someone a capitalist. The latest *COD* still says that a *capitalist* is 'someone who possesses capital' which applies to a lot of people. But now Karl Marx has won and most people object to being called *capitalists* because they would feel accused of exploiting the people who work for them. These days *capitalists* prefer to be called 'industrialists'.

... I consider an understanding of language an essential prerequisite for an 'ethically' just society ....
Arnold Wesker, *Words as Definitions of Experience*

capital letters
Some years ago many words were automatically given the dignity of a capital letter: Managing Director, the Police, Civil Servant, Bishop, Bank Manager. As part of our more relaxed attitude towards authority, these words would now usually begin with a small letter: managing director, the police, etc. Prime Minister still takes a capital when she or he is in office but not necessarily afterwards (Margaret Thatcher is a former prime minister). There is no general rule and often you can suit yourself, although it is useful to use a *capital* for the specific and a small letter for the general: 'The Bishop gave an address to the assembly of bishops.' See also **God** or **god**.

carefree or **careless**
There is an important distinction now. *Carefree* (a hyphen is not necessary) is a happy state, free from care or anxiety. *Careless* at one time meant the same (Elizabeth Barrett Browning: 'He never could recapture – The first fine careless rapture'). But now *careless* is nearly always used in a negative way, to mean not bothering, not giving a damn.

catalyst†
You will use this now fashionable word more effectively if you understand what it means in chemistry: a substance that, without changing itself, brings about a chemical change in something else. The extension of this meaning in

everyday language is for something or somebody who does or says very little but changes a situation or brings about an understanding simply by being present: 'A good counsellor can act as a *catalyst* in a difficult marital situation.'

catch-22†

Useful shorthand to describe a 'heads I lose – tails you win situation'. It is in dictionaries now although some, but not all, class it as 'slang'. It comes from Joseph Heller's book *Catch-22* in which a fighter pilot asks to be grounded because he is insane. But the proposed flight mission was suicidal and it was good sense to try to get out of it. So how could he be insane? Suppose your boss asks you to come up with a brilliant new idea. You do just that and he says 'But how do we know it will work – we've never tried anything like it before?' That's a *catch-22*.

Caucasian†

The Caucasus in the former USSR is where white races are supposed to have originated and *Caucasian* is occasionally a useful non-racist word that can be applied to white or light-skinned races. On a recent BBC *Today* programme a doctor described research being carried out on *Caucasians* to see if their response to specific drugs was different from Africans. Pron: 'kawKAYsian'. See **racist words**

ceiling and **floor**

It is easy to make a fool of yourself using these words to indicate the upper and lower limit of something. Philip Howard reminds us of a cabinet minister who wanted to put 'a *ceiling* price on carpets'. And I once heard a production manager, referring to a maximum price, saying 'I am determined to stick to the *ceiling*.'

Celsius†

Early in 1985, the BBC switched from giving temperatures in their weather forecasts as X° centigrade to X° *Celsius*. *Anders Celsius* (1701-44) was the Swedish astronomer who devised the logical centigrade scale at which water freezes at 0° and boils at 100°. *Celsius* (with a capital C) is the international name for this scale and is now adopted in the UK. There is nothing else to learn, because 20° *Celsius* is exactly the same as 20° centigrade and both are abbreviated 20°C (no stop). Pron: 'SELsyus'.

chairman or chairperson

Chairperson or *chair* is now standard usage on the BBC (the *chairperson* of quiz programmes) and committees everywhere now nearly always have *chairpersons* or *chairs* at the head. ICI and most other big institutions still prefer to have a *chairman* ... but just wait a few more years. See **sexist language**

chamber or chamber-

Chamber-maid (with a hyphen), *chamber-pot* (also with a hyphen) but never a hyphen for *chamber music*.

chap

Chap (formerly an abbreviation for 'chapman', a kind of travelling salesman) is now a dated word for a man. Do women go out with *chaps* any more? *Old chap* now sounds patronizing and *chappie* is coy.

Where now are the debs, gold-diggers, and flappers, not to mention the belles and vamps, who used to lead a chap on and then give him the air? Where are the roués, the triflers, the philanderers, the rakes, the cads, and the gigolos? .... When did the last young couple neck, pet or spoon .... When did you last meet an old maid?

Willard R. Espy, *Words at Play*

charisma and charismatic†

A fashionable word but it is better to use it sparingly, always remembering that it originally meant a quality conferred by God. We should reserve it for some extra-ordinary indefinable quality about a person that sets them apart and enables them to have exceptional influence on others. There are people like that but not many of them. Pron: 'kaRISma' and 'karisMATic'.

chauvinism and chauvinist

Nicolas Chauvin, a passionate follower of Napoleon, gave his name to this dangerous unthinking kind of blind patriotism: 'my country, my party, my cause – right or wrong'. The women's liberation movement took over the word and used it for men who deny women an equal place in society. Both meanings now exist in dictionaries and to avoid confusion *male chauvinist* is used by women's lib or, more abusively, *male chauvinist pig*.

check or **check up on** and **check out**

Everyone agrees that it's all right to *check* something. Some nitpickers object to *check up on* as an unnecessary import from the US. But many people like using *check up on* to imply checking extra carefully because there is doubt. And these days we *check out* of hotels, in England as well as America.

check or **cheque**

You write *cheques* in the UK and *checks* in America.

chief executive

Very few British companies still prefer 'managing director' for *chief executive*, used in American business, is now standard in the UK, led by the Post Office, which sacrificed the splendid title 'Postmaster General' by changing it to the 'Chairman and *Chief Executive* of the Post Office Board'. Nowadays some chief executives bask in the title *CEO* (for chief executive officer).

childish or **childlike**

It is a pity to mix up these words, as often happens, since to be *childlike* is to have the natural innocence and openness of a child, a quality that makes every day an adventure, whereas to be *childish* is to be immature, spoilt and stupid.

class

This has become a touchy word since the egalitarian revolution of the 1960s and now most people of all 'classes' are nervous about using the word *class*. When Jilly Cooper set out to write a book about the English class system, 'people drew away from me in horror' she said. Advertising agencies get round it by referring to 'socio-economic groups' but for the rest of us, *class* has become almost a taboo word. Under Margaret Thatcher's jurisdiction, some people went back to talking about the different *classes* but that is no longer comfortable. If you cannot dismiss the whole business as irrelevant, you have to find new words to express social differences or fall back on 'working-class', 'upper middle-class' and so on, although the tide is flowing against you.

It has become impossible to define class. Twenty years ago, belonging to a golf club was a guarantee of middle-class status. Now it's a favourite sport of taxi drivers. Soccer used to be the preserve of the Sun-reading class. Today you can't get in at Arsenal without showing your Guardian.

Barry Hugill in the *Guardian*

class language

In the 1950s, a linguistic scholar, Professor A.S.C. Ross, became well-known when he analysed 'upper-class' (*U*) and 'non-upper-class' (*Non-U*) English. Is it all still relevant? You might hear *U* English at Ascot (but don't count on it) or on the playing fields of Eton or in clubs in Pall Mall (don't count on that either). Some of Professor Ross's *Non-U* expressions were: 'don't give up', 'it's as simple as that', 'it's just one of those things', 'I'll go along with that', 'back to square one'. But before you drop any of those, remember they are used in both Houses of Parliament, Oxford and Cambridge senior common rooms and by many educated literary men and women living in the UK. If it exists in the 21st century, *U* English is a kind of dialect of particular words, pronunciations and locutions, affected by certain people. It has nothing to do with the quality of words or using them sensitively or intelligently. See **accents**

cleavage

Words have a will of their own and *cleavage*, which has technical meanings such as the splitting of a molecule into simpler molecules, is accepted as standard English in *COD* for 'the space between a woman's breasts' (this usage is still classified 'colloq.' by some dictionaries). There is no other word for it anyway.

clichés

The sad thing about *clichés* (phrases that have become used too often by too many) is that good vivid expressions are killed off by over-use. Suppose you wrote this: I 'have seen better days', am 'poor but honest' and 'haven't slept a wink' because someone has 'made me mad'; if something is 'all Greek to you' or simply 'neither here nor there'; when 'there is method in your madness' and 'last but not least', 'to tell the truth and shame the devil', 'your heart's desire' is to 'have a charmed life' and to be 'as sound as a bell', because it is 'cold comfort' to be told 'you can only die once' ... you would be accused of using a whole string of *clichés*. Yet every one of those phrases was written by the greatest of all manipulators of English words, Shakespeare. Do we now have to discard them? We do have to be careful about using them, because custom has made them stale. But they can still make a lively contribution to what we say or write whenever we find a fresh unexpected way of giving them new life.

client or **customer**

Solicitors, accountants, advertising agencies, insurance brokers, etc. all have *clients*, so do some hairdressers (the posh ones have a *clientele*). Shops have *customers* although couturiers and the grander dress-shops give themselves airs by having *clients*. As Eric Partridge says, 'What's wrong with *customer*, anyway?' and for the whole lot of them at that.

climax

Some scholars still stupidly fight well-established usage, arguing that *climax* comes from the Greek word meaning 'ladder' and should be used to mean an advancing sequence. But everyone and all dictionaries take it now to mean the most dramatic or most critical point in a situation.

climb up and **climb down**

It is pompous to object, as some do, to *climb up* because 'up' is the only direction you can climb. Language conveys feeling as well as fact and 'up' adds to the feeling of upward movement. As for criticizing *climb down* because the two words are contradictory, whoever said that effective use of language should always be strictly logical? We all say *climb down* because it conveys more effectively a feeling of effort and movement than the alternative 'descend'. It is also a useful phrase to describe someone who has had to admit defeat or reverse an opinion: 'The dispute was settled out of court after a dramatic *climb-down* by one of the parties.'

co or co-

Most *co* words do not need a hyphen. Some exceptions: 1. Usually when the next word begins with 'o': co-operate (but note 'uncooperative'), co-opt, co-ordinate (but 'uncoordinated'). 2. When you need a hyphen to help with the pronunciation: co-latitude, co-religionist. 3. Several words where *co-* is used for a person sharing an activity with someone else: co-author, co-pilot, co-star and even co-husband and co-wife.

cock**

A linguistic reflection of sexual inhibitions is the many hang-ups over words for our sexual organs. The Latin names are the polite ones, 'penis' for the male organ or even more formally, 'membrum virile'; and 'pudendum' or 'pudendum muliebre' for a woman's genitals. The moment you leave those expressions behind, you are in trouble, because the alternatives are 'vulgar' words. *Cock*** is the most common word, used by both men and women, for a man's sexual organ; and 'cunt'*** is the word often used for a woman's. The linguistic scholar, Eric Partridge, said this about such words: 'The Saxon words for the male member and the female pudendum are excellently idiomatic and belong to the aristocracy of the language ....' But these are words that can shock people. *Genitals*, for both sexes, is an alternative acceptable even to the prudish. To *talk cock*, meaning nonsense, and a *cock-up*, meaning a complete mess of something, are considered 'slang' by dictionaries but not 'vulgar'; both expressions are used in conversation and it would be rare for someone to object.

collective words

Words such as *board*, *company*, *committee*, *class* (in a school), *department*, cover a group of people or things (a *fleet* of ships). The problem is whether to treat them as singular or plural. A number of these words are listed in this book, as they occur alphabetically. The problem is dealt with under the entry for **board**.

collusion

Avoid using this word in a *good* sense: 'The two scientists are working in *collusion* on the experiments.' The proper word there is 'co-operation' or 'collaboration' because *collusion* is always used about something crooked: 'The directors are in *collusion* over cooking the accounts.'

colony

The words *colony* and *colonial* are now dirty words, reeking of imperialism and exploitation. Instead *colonies* are now called 'dependent territories' which comes to the same thing but sounds better.

coloured

See **black** and **racist words**

comedian or **comic**

These words overlap but generally a *comedian* is a 'serious' comic, an actor who plays a comedy role in plays or films or sketches. You expect a *comic* to be broader, more of a clown. Women are not usually called *comics* and no matter how way-out their style of comedy, they are *comediennes*.

commercial

Of course this word has a perfectly harmless and legitimate use but it has come to carry with it the suggestion of being more interested in profits than in quality and integrity: 'the *commercial* theatre', 'too commercial'. It was a linguistic master-stroke to call the *commercial* TV service in the UK 'independent television' but the advertising agencies missed a trick when they did not call *commercials* 'announcements'. *Commercial* is a word to be careful about. See **psycholinguistics**

commie

This slang word for a communist has given way to the more serious word 'Marxist'. 'Fellow-traveller' was at one time used for someone who sympathizes with but is not an official member of the Communist Party.

committee

See **board**

common

A *common* man can mean a man of the people or a man who is coarse and uncouth. It is perhaps becoming less usual to talk about someone as being *common*, meaning unrefined and vulgar, and when the American composer,

Aaron Copland, called his composition *Fanfare for the Common Man*, this was also the right title in the UK. Do not take it for granted that everyone will always understand what you mean by *common*: 'Our common friend' could mean a friend you have in common with someone else *or* your uncouth friend! Keep the word 'mutual' in reserve to prevent misunderstanding. See **mutual**

communal and **commune**

Pronounce it 'COMmunal' not 'comMUNal'. If you live on a *commune*, call it a 'COMmune' but if you *commune* with nature, then you can either 'COMmune' or 'comMUNE' with it (the latter is more usual).

company

See **board**

comparable

Pronounce it 'COMparable'; 'comPARable' is often heard but is still considered 'wrong'.**

complete

It is rightly said that *complete* is an absolute quality so something cannot be 'more complete' than something else. In some situations, it is acceptable to have degrees of *completeness*: 'This is the most *complete* account of what has happened.' But it is better to avoid saying that something is 'very complete', as that makes a nonsense of the word.

complex

In psychology, a complex is an interacting group of unconscious tendencies that pathologically affect our responses and behaviour. The trouble started when the Austrian psychiatrist, Alfred Adler, invented the term *inferiority complex*, since when everyone has a *complex* about something. For now we use *complex* for any marked tendency or strong feeling in ourselves or someone else, without it being necessarily morbid or neurotic: 'You've got a *complex* about being on time.' More recently, *complex* is used more and more about an arrangement of buildings in a contained area (a 'shopping complex'). A '*complex* situation', a '*complex* problem' and so on implies that the situation or problem has a number of different factors connected with it. Otherwise it would be clearer to use 'complicated'.

compound

To '*compound* a felony' (pron: 'comPOUND') is a formal

legal charge that you have deliberately concealed or refrained from prosecuting in the case of a crime committed by someone. This has led people to use *compound* in a confusing way to mean making something worse: 'You have *compounded* the mistake by making another mistake.' It would be clearer to say 'You have added to the mistake ....' Other and rarer uses of *compound* are listed in dictionaries.

comprise

Means almost exactly the same as 'consist of' but you do not use 'of' after comprised: 'The Group *comprises* six companies' (not 'is *comprised* of'); 'the orchestra, *comprising* 60 musicians ...' (not '*comprised* of').

comptroller

This old-fashioned word, based on a mistaken spelling (through a wrong association with Latin 'computus') that caught on 400 years ago, still survives for some official titles: 'Comptroller-General of the National Debt Office'. It sounds grand but don't be impressed because it means *exactly* the same and is pronounced exactly the same as controller.

computer-aided

This applies to a number of different processes which make use of a visual display screen linked to a computer. The most usual ones are computer-aided design (designs made directly on to a screen instead of on paper, so that they can be worked on electronically), and computer-aided manufacturing (which uses computers to control every stage of manufacture).

computer crime

This is so-called 'white collar' crime involving unauthorized use of a computer system. Computer crime is electronic forgery, used to carry out fraudulent fund transfers, to manipulate data or gain access to confidential information.

concept

These days *concept* (once a developed theory based on observed instances) is used all the time to make quite ordinary ideas seem significant and important. Do not be taken in by it. After all, *concept* can now mean no more than 'something conceived in the mind' (*LD*), whether it makes sense or not.

conjugal

Marital problems are ever on the increase, but at least we can be clear about how to pronounce *conjugal*, the word for the state of being married: 'CONjoogle'.

connection or connexion

Either. But connection is the usual spelling.

consummate

When it is pronounced 'conSUMat', it means altogether perfect: 'a *consummate* performance'. When you say 'CONsermayt' it means to complete something (a marriage is *consummated* by sexual intercourse).

contact

A few die-hards are still saying that you cannot *contact* anyone, you can only make a *contact*. Ivor Brown (in *A Word in Your Ear*) took a more reasonable view as far back as the early 1940s: 'There is no other word which covers approach by telephone, letter and speech, and *contact* is self-explanatory and concise.'

contagious or infectious

Most people know the difference but it could be dangerous not to be quite clear. A *contagious* disease is one you can catch only by direct physical contact with someone or something. You can catch an *infectious* disease by air or water. Apart from disease, the words are used interchangeably: 'his enthusiasm was contagious', 'her laughter was infectious'.

continual or continuous

There is a useful distinction to be kept. *Continual* refers to something that is going on all the time but with interruptions. *Continuous* is going on all the time without interruption. It is hardly possible to argue *continuously* all day; you have to stop sometimes. But there can be a 'continuous buzz'.

contracted forms

I'm, I'll, you're, you'll, isn't, it's, can't, don't, he's, she's, they're ... We all use them in conversation but some people hesitate to use them in writing. Written English and spoken English are much closer to each other now and these contractions appear in official letters from doctors, solicitors, MPs and from many others who would not have used them at one time. Respected novelists, such as William Trevor, Saul Bellow and Martin Amis, use them, not only in dialogue, where they are natural, but also in descriptive prose. When it seems laboured to write these forms out in full repeatedly, the way is now wide open to use the contractions, even in formal letters. But remember that if you overdo it, it can look sloppy. 'I'd', 'you'd', 'he'd', 'she'd', 'we'd' sound perfectly all right when we say them but still look a little odd in print so, although there's no rule about it, they're not used in writing as often as the other contracted forms.

controversy

It depends upon how much you care what people think. The safe pronunciation puts the stress on the *first* syllable: CONtroversy. 'ConTROversy' is shown as an alternative pronunciation in most modern dictionaries but is sometimes regarded as ill-educated.

cool

The use of *cool* by American jazz musicians to mean restrained or unemotional passed into standard English years ago. The slang expression 'laid-back' has taken over for that meaning, and cool is mostly used now simply as an expression of approval, more or less as a synonym for 'Great!'

coronary

Sadly what was once a rare word has become much more in

use because of the increasing occurrence of *coronary thrombosis*, the blocking of an artery to the heart. Doctors put the stress on the *first* syllable and pronounce it 'CORronery'.

cosmonaut or **astronaut**

See **astronaut**

cost-effective

A useful expression to define achieving something at a cost that makes good sense in relation to what is achieved: 'This is a *cost-effective* way of introducing the new model.' It should imply good value for money but look at it carefully whenever you see it because it can cover up a waste of money: something can be called *cost-effective* but may cost much more than is necessary.

councillor or **counsellor**

It doesn't matter when you are talking, because they both sound the same. In writing, you have to be careful. A *councillor* is a member of a council, nowadays usually in local government. A *counsellor* is someone who gives advice ('marriage-guidance counsellor') and the advice they give is 'counsel'. Barristers are, of course, called 'counsels', not *counsellors*. The following sounds confusing when you say it but not when you read it: 'The Council consulted a counsel.'

It is one thing to use language; it is quite another to understand how it works.

Anthony Burgess, *Joysprick*

countdown†

This method, used in space and nuclear technology, of counting second by second backwards to zero seems logical because it tells us how many seconds we have left. But left before *what*?

counter-productive

When you take measures to achieve something and they produce the *opposite* result, that's *counter-productive* ... and very discouraging.

cowboy

Cowboys used to be good people but the slang use of the word *cowboy*, understandably frequent these days, is for someone who makes a botch of anything, from repairing your plumbing to a business deal, in order to make a quick buck. Look out for that kind of *cowboy*!

credibility gap†

Useful linguistic shorthand to say there is a difference between what is said or written and what seem to be the facts.

crescendo

Should be used in relation only to *sounds* which get louder and louder to reach a climax. It is a standard musical term. We should try to avoid using *crescendo* sloppily as in 'It is the *crescendo* of his achievement.' The better word there is climax. See **climax**

criterion

We still use the classical plural: one *criterion*, two or more *criteria*.

culture

'Australian culture' can mean the arts in Australia or it could mean the pattern of behaviour, thoughts, institutions and so on, that is the entire Australian life-style. Where there is risk of misunderstanding, use the words 'the arts' or 'life-style' instead.

cutback

There is a *cutback* (one word) in production but production has been *cut back* (two words). You could say, as some do, that *back* is unnecessary and that it's enough to say that production (or whatever) has been *cut*. Nevertheless, *back* has a certain emotional force and emphasizes the negative aspect of a *cutback*.

cute

Unless you want to sound like a middle-aged American tourist, goggle-eyed at European customs, it would be better to drop this word.

D

dago

At one time used harmlessly in the US for a Latin-American Spaniard (*Diego* is the Spanish equivalent of 'James'). Then it deteriorated into an abusive slang name for almost any foreigner but especially for Spaniards, Italians and Portuguese. Do not use it now unless you want a fight.

dame

Some men, especially in the US, still talk about 'having dinner with a dame', but it now sounds dated, unless you are having dinner with a Dame (capital D), who in the UK is a female member of an order of knighthood.

dashes

The rule for some writers is – when in doubt use a *dash*: 'So I said to this feller – see – if that's really what you want to do – well then – you'd better get on with it – and what do you think? – he *did*!' The result may be clear but it's the literary equivalent of gobbling your food. You can use a *dash* as an alternative to a *colon* :, which is what I'm about to do, and in addition there are at least three other useful functions – 1. Dashes can separate a phrase from the rest of the sentence: 'I was leaving for the office – early that morning as it happens – when the telephone rang.' 2. To follow something up: 'It was one of the kindest things you could have done – to ask me out to dinner that evening.' 3. To gather up a list of things and re-present them: 'Income-tax, a mortgage, instalments on the car, renting a TV – by the time you've paid all those, there's not much left.'

data is or data are

In order to demonstrate that you know that in Latin *datum* is singular and *data* is plural, it is the done thing to say 'a lot of data *are* available'. In America, or if you work in *data* processing, you may be more at home with 'data *is* available'. Say 'data are' and someone will say you are a pedantic fusspot: change to 'data is' and someone else may say you're an ignorant nit. That's the state of play these days. At least you are safe to pronounce it 'dayta', as the BBC do, rather than 'datta' or 'dahta', which are not recommended.

daughter-in-laws or **daughters-in-law**

If you want to keep up with Mrs Jones next door, be sure to say *daughters-in-law* which is the correct plural.

deadline

In the 19th century this was a line round a military prison beyond which a prisoner might be shot. In its more recent meaning of an absolute time-limit, it is now one of the words on which the fate of the world may hang. When someone gives you a *deadline*, as I was with this book, by which something must be ready or agreed, you know they mean business.

deadly or **deathly**

Something that is *deadly* can kill you (a *deadly* poison). *Deathly* is like death: 'a *deathly* silence' (as quiet as the grave) or 'a *deathly* pallor'. When a left-handed spinner delivers *deadly* bowling, batsmen cannot cope; and something can be *deadly* dull (so dull it almost bores you to death).

... when I start a sentence in which I am trying to express something very important to me, the words on the page assume a new life, semi-independent of their life in my head. Having written something down, it is no longer true.

Andy, a sixth-form student, Schools Council Project, *The Role of English*

de-

de- has been used since the Middle Ages to make a word mean the opposite but in recent years this has become an epidemic, as it is a convenient shorthand that suits bureaucratic pomposity. You can go into hospital and be 'hospitalized' and then when you're cured, *de-hospitalized*. Margaret Thatcher's policy was to 'privatize' things and some opposition MPs threatened to *de-privatize* them, possibly because it seemed more like 'talking tough' than 're-nationalize'. If you feel like it, you can jump on the bandwagon and invent new *de-* words for yourself: *The Times* has referred to *de-education* (presumably unlearning something), an MP has said he will *de-resign* (that is withdraw his resignation), and someone I know, who doesn't like 'divorce', said she was going to get *de-married*.

Sometimes, when a *de-* word becomes familiar, the hyphen is dropped as in 'declassify' (to take something off the secret list), but there's no reliable rule about this. See **hyphens**

decade

When you say it aloud stress the *first* syllable: 'DECade'.

defect

Some dictionaries recommend 'DEEfect' as the pronunciation, others 'diFFECT' and others give you the choice, which in fact you have. But the second pronunciation ('diFFECT', with stress on *second* syllable) is the right one to describe someone leaving one political party or one country to ally themselves with another ('He *defected* to the West').

defective or **deficient**

It is safer to use *defective* to describe something that doesn't work properly and *deficient* for when an essential part is missing, even though most dictionaries are woolly about this distinction (the most recent Oxford dictionary defines *defective* as 'lacking or deficient').

definite

Avoid spelling it 'definate'**, a common mistake. It means clear and well defined: 'It's a *definite* proposal.' But it is so often used, especially in conversation, when you're sure about something: 'Do you love me?' '*Definitely*!'; 'I *definitely* think …' (meaning there is no doubt about what I think). You could argue that this strays from the proper meaning of *definite*, but you'd have to work hard to avoid using it that way. Does it matter? In my view, *definitely* not.

definite or **definitive**

A *definitive* answer is a final answer, and that's that. A *definite* answer means a clear unambiguous answer (although many people would use it to mean an answer that they are sure about – see **definite** above). A *definite* offer is a positive offer whereas a *definitive* offer is a final offer – not a penny more (but they may be bluffing of course).

deflower

It seems strange, in the 21st century, to use this old-worldly 14th-century expression, but it is still perhaps the only way we have to describe the act of taking away a woman's virginity. *Deflower* is still used, although rarely now, and the implication that something beautiful and innocent has been lost has not altogether disappeared.

delusion or **illusion**

A *delusion* is a feeling of certainty that something false is true ('to labour under a delusion'). An *illusion* is something imaginary, not founded on reality. Both words are similar in meaning, although *delusions* can be more dangerous and in extreme cases can be a form of madness. Most of us have some illusions and it would be hard to live without them. In practice, it is not likely to matter much if you mix these words up but be careful: 'He has so many delusions' means he is wrong about so many things with the implication that this could do a lot of harm; 'He has so many illusions' means he lives in cloud-cuckoo-land and is probably harmless enough.

democrat

It can mean two things. The political meaning is someone who believes in government by the people: one man –

one vote. It is also used now to mean believing in the absence of hereditary 'class' distinction and the influence of wealth. Many people, who are *democrats* in the former sense, are very far from being *democrats* in the more recent sense of the word, and have unshakeable 'them and us' feelings. With a capital D, *Democrat* means specifically a member of the Democratic Party in the US.

dependant or dependent

Don't worry if you have to think twice – a lot of people do. It's this way round: you can claim tax relief for a *dependant*, but the rate of relief is *dependent* on your income.

despatch or dispatch

One book on 'correct' English states: '*despatch* is correct, but *dispatch* is now much more normal'. Wouldn't you prefer to be 'normal'? In any case, the latest 'Oxford' point of view prefers *dispatch*, so you can have it both ways.

détente

Although all it means is a state of relaxation ('a moment of détente') it came to be used almost exclusively about the relationship between the US and the former USSR. When they were at least talking to one another, there was – *détente*. Pronounce it the French way ('dayTAHNT') and put an accent over the '*é*'.

detour

Some say 'DAYtour', others 'DEEtour' and some people couldn't care less, which is sensible because both are 'correct'. Americans say 'deTOUR'.

developing country

The earlier expression *underdeveloped country* is felt to be condescending, and the United Nations now prefers the more euphemistic term *developing country*, suggesting the process of changing over to an industrial base.

deviant

It used to mean someone whose behaviour was out of the ordinary but I'd advise you not to use it that way any more, since it is now commonly used by heterosexuals about homosexuals and lesbians, and conveys a negative undertone.

devil's advocate

It is easy to see why this expression, still much used these days, is often misunderstood. The *devil's advocate* was the official in the papal court who found objections to someone being declared a saint. In everyday use, it means someone who picks holes in something that is positive and constructive. Suppose you are planning to present proposals to a client. A colleague might say 'Let me be the *devil's advocate*.' That is, they will put up all possible objections to your proposals, so that when you face the client you will be ready with the answers.

diagnosis or **prognosis**

When these medical terms are used more generally, they are sometimes confused. A doctor *diagnoses* a disease, that is, he works out what is wrong with the patient. The doctor's *prognosis* is a forecast of how the disease will develop. Likewise a problem in business, or any other sphere, is *diagnosed* when we find out the real cause; our *prognosis* might be that it will sort itself out or that the business will go bust.

didn't

See **contracted forms**

different

A word that has a way of slipping in where it's not wanted: 'He has had three *different* wives', 'He looked it up in six *different* books.' A moment's thought and you can see that in such sentences *different* means nothing at all.

Listening to the eight o'clock news on the wireless this morning, I was appalled to hear that two infinitives had been split within three minutes of each other.

Letter to the BBC, quoted by
David Crystal on Radio 4

different from, to or **than**

Can anyone say anything new about this old grammatical chestnut? Let me at least put my cards on the table: all three forms can be considered 'correct'; it is a matter of how it sounds to you. For some people, *different from* is the only acceptable form and they object even to *different to*, although nearly all current dictionaries list it, not only as good English, but as the more usual form (after all, we say 'opposed to', 'dissimilar to'). *Different than** makes some people hot under the collar yet it is almost standard usage in America, has been used by good writers in the

UK (Oliver Goldsmith and the economist John Maynard Keynes are just two examples) and is convenient in a sentence such as 'Things are very *different* in New York *than* in London.' Which form you use, or whether you use all three, depends upon how much you mind a few die-hards criticizing your grammar.

dilemma

You have not got the hang of this word if you say 'We're in a *dilemma* about where to go for our holiday.' To be in a *dilemma* is to be between the devil and the deep blue sea, that is to be faced by two *nasty* alternatives: 'I'm in a *dilemma* over whether to pay the phone bill or have it cut off.' Oxford dictionaries offer a choice of pronunciation: either 'dilLEMMa' (first syllable rhymes with 'pill') or 'dieLEMMa'.

dipsomaniac

You will not hear doctors talking about anyone being a *dipsomaniac*, just as it would sound very old-fashioned to talk about an 'inebriate'. Both those words mean someone addicted to drink, but now you would say they're 'alcoholics'.

direct

Current dictionaries give a choice of pronunciation: you can go *direct* (the first syllable rhyming with the first syllable of 'mirror') or you can pronounce it 'dieRECT'. You have the same choice when you go off in any *direction*, if you are the *director* of a company, or look something up in a *directory*. But once you've made up your mind, keep to the same pronunciation for the first syllable of all four words.

dirty words

Because humankind finds it difficult to reconcile its higher intelligence with its animal functions, the ordinary words for those functions are labelled *dirty words*. Add to that the hangover from Victorian repressiveness and we are left hedged in on all sides whenever we want to talk about our fundamental bodily activities. Havelock Ellis's *Studies in the Psychology of Sex* was declared 'lewd and obscene' by the courts in 1897; over a century later, the English language still maintains much the same conspiracy of silence. The ways some women and men make love to each other remain shrouded in the 'decent' obscurity of Latin words, such as 'fellatio' and 'cunnilingus', and the moment we attempt to lift the veil, we have to use so-called *dirty words*. Whether we go along with this game or take a more open linguistic attitude depends upon our hang-ups or how much we care about offending others. See **four-letter words**.

The word 'sex', abused and smutted into a horrible nightmare, was abandoned altogether, and for 'sexual intercourse' he substituted 'the genital embrace'.
Paul Robinson, *The Sexual Radicals*

disasterous or **disastrous**

-erous is the usual ending in such words (murderous, slanderous, etc.). *Disastrous* and *wondrous* are two common exceptions.

disc or **disk**

The 1959 *Shorter Oxford Dictionary* recommended *disk*. This has now been reversed and most current dictionaries prefer *disc*, relegating *disk* to American usage. But *disk* is always used, even in the UK, in connection with computers. Compact *disc* or *disk* has become a free for all. Because they are used in computers, compact *disk* is taking over. Either way, it's a very long time since anyone put on a *record*.

discount

Fritz Spiegl, a commentator on the use of English, once complained about BBC newsreaders who '*dis*count the possibility, instead of dis*count*ing it, as if they were talking about cut-price socks'. He's right of course: we '*dis*COUNT' (stress on second syllable) something when we write it off as being untrue or unimportant; but when we buy something for less than the going rate, we get a '*DIS*count' (stress on first syllable).

disinterested or **uninterested**

A judge should always be *disinterested*, that is he should be impartial and not take sides. But if he is *uninterested*, he might doze off, because that would mean he is bored by the proceedings. The trouble with these two words is that you cannot always be sure that someone else will understand even when you use them correctly. Most people know that *an interested party* is someone with a financial stake in something, so when in doubt, you can substitute for *disinterested*, 'I am not an interested party.'

disorientated or **disoriented**

Both are 'correct' although some people feel that *disoriented* is American usage. Nevertheless *disoriented* is taking over in the UK because it's easier to say.

dispute

BBC newsreaders, who are always having to talk about *disputes*, are advised to stress the second syllable (disPUTE) whether it's a *dispute* or someone *disputes* something. The same applies to *disputable* (say 'disPUTEable').

distrait or **distraught**

If you are *distrait* (pron: 'disTRAY') your mind is elsewhere, usually because you're a little worried about something. But if you are *distraught* (pron: 'diSTRAWT') it means you are worried sick.

distribute

Although you sometimes hear it said with the stress on the first syllable (DIStribute), the standard pronunciation is to stress the second: disTRIBute.

... pronunciation is a highly personal matter. Like bridge, croquet, and back-seat driving, it may cause arguments between husband and wife.

Willard R. Espy, *Words at Play*

doesn't

See **contracted forms**

dolce vita

Using foreign expressions unnecessarily can sound affected, but *la dolce vita*, which came our way in the 1960s from Fellini's film of that name, is justified because there's no good alternative in English. The 'good life' suggests a life of quality and happiness, whereas *la dolce vita* is out-and-out self-indulgence, taking whatever pleasure you fancy and to hell with other people.

don't

See **contracted forms**

double entendre

This linguistic curiosity sounds French, of course, but is not used in France, so don't try it over there. It appeared in English in the 17th century and is now standard English, useful for describing one of those expressions that sound innocent enough but which also have an unmistakable sexual meaning. *Double entendres* are an underhand way of making sexually suggestive remarks.

double-talk and **double-think**†

Double-talk, a good expression from the US, refers to claptrap that appears to make good sense, or which is deliberately ambiguous, so that you cannot be sure what it means. George Orwell in his novel, *1984*, extended the idea to *double-think* to describe the ability to believe in two ideas, even though they contradict each other. Both expressions are now accepted as standard English.

downside

Although not yet in some recent dictionaries, *downside* is a word now frequently used in connection with investments. The *downside risk* is an estimate of the most you can lose, so you know where you stand even if things go badly wrong.

draft or **draught**

It is so easy to get mixed up over which to use and even

some dictionaries seem confused. In the UK, we *draft* legal documents, treaties, a letter, a preliminary sketch for a design, or a plan for carrying out a project. The legal document, treaty, etc. becomes a *draft*. But we prefer *draught* beer and do not like sitting in a *draught*. In the US, *draft* is the preferred spelling for all those uses. In the UK, a *draftsman* or *draftswoman* draws up legal documents and a *draughtsman* or *draughtswoman* does drawings. In America, they tend to use *draughtsman/draughtswoman* for both. It sounds complicated but the above guidelines are reliable, even though you will come across variations on both sides of the Atlantic. One last point: a game of draughts in the UK is a game of 'checkers' in America.

drag

The slang meanings may seem puzzling. A man in woman's clothing is in *drag* – but *not* the other way round. This usage goes back much further than people think: in the mid-19th century, *drag* referred to the long petticoats (which dragged along the ground) worn by actors in women's roles. When someone or something is a drag, they are boring, heavy-going, and this is a good vivid slang expression: 'He's such a *drag* at parties.'

drank or **drunk**

If this is a problem, remember this sentence: 'I *drink* today, I *drank* yesterday and last week I was *drunk*.'

drawing

The problem is one of pronunciation and it is called 'the intrusive r', a light -r- sound creeping in: 'draw-r-ing', 'I saw-r-it', 'awe-r-inspiring'. There is nothing new about this and in the 19th century the philologist, Henry Sweet, drew attention to 'The India-r-Office'. In very formal speech perhaps we should avoid 'the intrusive r' as it could make us sound too casual. But in everyday rapid conversation it is so common that even the most literary speakers are content to let the -r- slip in from time to time. Be aware of it but don't let it keep you awake at nights.

dreamed or **dreamt**

Either will do: 'I *dreamed* last night' or 'I *dreamt* last night.' But note that *dreamt* is heard less than it used to be, and *dreamed* is more usual now.

due to

Thousands of words have been written in grammar books to explain that *due to* must always be used as an 'adjective' and that instead of saying '*Due to* illness he was absent' we must say 'His absence was *due to* illness' so that *due to* 'qualifies' the word 'absence'. The grammatical explanation is not at all easy for everyone to follow and many good writers feel that nothing important is lost if they use *due to* in the same way as 'because of' or 'owing to': 'Play was stopped *due to* rain', '*Due to* a breakdown in negotiations, the strike started.' But be aware that a few people might consider those sentences 'ungrammatical' and insist on 'The stoppage of play was *due to* ...', 'The starting of the strike was *due to* ....' Nevertheless, some experienced writers now adopt the 'Play was stopped *due to* ...'* usage which leaves the way open for you to do the same.

Grammar to a writer is a total irrelevance. If I start thinking about grammar, I get caught up in the how *instead of the* what ... *grammar is a stranglehold on passion. But before a writer discards grammar, he must know it intimately. He must at one time have loved it. He must always respect it. Only then is its irrelevance clear and logical.*

Bernice Rubens, the first woman writer
to win the Booker Prize

E

each

If you are ever uncertain about whether *each* is singular ('each has ...', etc.) or plural ('each have ...', etc.) here is a neat rule: when *each* comes before the word it refers to, treat it as singular: '*Each* of them is ...', '*Each* of the players was ....' When *each* comes after the word it refers to, it is plural: 'They each *were* ...', 'London and New York each *have* many good restaurants.' *Each one*, of course, is always singular: 'Each one of the women is ....'

each other or one another

Some linguistic experts believe there is no justification for the rule, laid down in some books, that *each other* refers to two persons or things, and *one another* to more than two. So you can please yourself and say 'They love *each* other' or 'They love *one another*.'

earned or earnt

Unlike 'learned' and 'learnt', there is no choice. The only 'correct' form is *earned*.

east

See **north, south, east** and **west**

eatable or edible

You often hear these confused. *Edible* means safe to eat ('an *edible* mushroom'); *eatable* implies that the taste is good enough. So something that is *edible* may, if it's badly cooked, be *uneatable*. Be on guard against restaurants that do not know the difference between *eatable* and *edible*.

economic or economical

When it's cheap at the price, or at least good value, always use *economical*. Otherwise the proper word is *economic*. Economical is to do with economy (an 'economical car'), stretching pounds or dollars as far as possible. 'Economic' *always* relates to *economics*, the science of the production and distribution of wealth. But note that 'uneconomic' and 'uneconomical' are interchangeable, both meaning bad value for money. There is a choice of pronunciation of the 'e': like the 'e' in 'egg' ('ecknomic') or like 'ee' ('eekonomic').

ecstasy or extasy

A century or so ago, *extasy* was an accepted spelling but

now it is always *ecstasy*. *Ecstasy* is an overwhelming feeling of joy.

ecumenical

This is a confusing word to many people. Ecumenical used to describe the universal Christian Church, but is now taken to mean the movement to re-establish Christian unity, cutting across the different divisions. The new church in Milton Keynes symbolizes this ecumenical belief that the way ahead must be bridges across denominational divides. It is owned jointly by the Baptist Union, the Church of England, and the Methodist, Roman Catholic and United Reformed Church.

-ed

When one lawyer wants to sneer at another, he calls him 'my *learn-ed* friend' (giving the word two syllables). If you have spent a lifetime studying, you are also entitled to two syllables because you are 'learn-ed'. In the 15th century, *-ed* was nearly always pronounced as a separate syllable and with a few words this has lingered on, for some usages. See **beloved** and be careful every 'bless-ed' time you use the word *blessed*.

effect or **affect**

See **affect**

effing

By social convention, 'fucking' is an indecent word, shunned by polite society (although not by everyone), while *effing* (an acknowledged variant of 'fucking') is

considered no worse than 'slang' in some dictionaries and
is more or less acceptable.

e.g. or i.e.

These Latinate abbreviations are, of course, a common part
of English – and useful, although they get mixed up sometimes. *e.g.* (Latin: *exempli gratia*) is simply shorthand for
'for example', and is usually preceded by a comma: 'There
is a wide choice on the menu, e.g. steak, trout and chicken.'
i.e. (Latin: *id est*), also preceded by a comma, is shorthand
for 'that is to say': 'There are only three main courses on
the menu, i.e. steak, trout and chicken.' Some people use
e.g. and *i.e.* in speech, which is both unnecessary and stupid.

Eire

In Gaelic, *Eire* (pron: 'airer' – without sounding the final 'r')
means Ireland and was adopted in 1937 as the official name
for the part of Ireland independent from the UK. Because of
the sensitive political situation, some people prefer not to
use *Eire* but to say the 'Republic of Ireland' (as proclaimed
on 18 April 1949) or more simply the Irish Republic.

either

Either is a minefield of difficulties. 1. Take care where
you put it: 'We shall either go to Paris or to Rome'
becomes more effective when *either* is repositioned – 'We
shall go to either Paris or Rome.' 2. Is *either* singular or
plural? If both words after *either* are singular, treat *either*
as singular: 'Either pilot error or mechanical failure *was*
to blame.' But if either of the words is plural, *either*
becomes plural: 'Either pilot error or the flight con-
trollers *were* to blame.' 3. In other cases, always look at
the *second* word related to *either*: 'Either he or *I am* to
blame', 'Either she or *you are* ....' 4. After all that, do you
say 'eyether' or 'eether'? *Either*! Dictionaries show *both*
as 'correct'. But in America it is *always* 'eether'.

elapse or lapse

Time elapses, that is passes by, just as hours or days can
elapse before we get down to work. We live in a time
when many customs and traditions *lapse*, that is fall into
disuse because nobody bothers with them any more. An
insurance policy can *lapse* if you don't pay the premium.

élitist

Not much more than perhaps 30 years ago, *élite* meant

the '*crème de la crème*', the upper-crust of society. Now the word *élite* has fallen to some extent out of favour because élitist has become a term of angry abuse for members of a small group wielding power as a result of unfair privilege.

emend or **amend**

See **amend**

emigrant or **immigrant**

Often mixed up, these are such sensitive words in society now, that we should get them right. The same person is usually both – but at different times: when people leave their own country for another, they are *emigrants*; when they arrive in the new country, they are *immigrants*. The word *emigrate* (to leave one's country) is a good way to remember.

empathy or **sympathy**

Empathy is a lovely word that more people are using now. It is the capacity to enter, in one's imagination, into someone else's feelings or into the whole mood and quality of a work of art. *Sympathy* is similar but always

includes compassion for suffering or distress. You have *empathy*, rather than *sympathy*, for a painting or a piece of music, and you may have *empathy* for someone in love, although *sympathy* could come in too, if you believe they are in love with the wrong person. Keep these words apart in your mind because they can be so rewarding and expressive to use. See **sympathetic**

enclose or **inclose**

They mean the same but inclose is on its way out. Stay with *enclose*.

enormity

When in February 1985 Neil Kinnock spoke of the *enormity* of the unemployment total in the UK, we weren't sure what he meant. It might have been the monstrousness, the sheer wickedness of the figures, because that is the true meaning of *enormity* ('the full *enormity* of a crime'). Or he might have been following a more recent usage, to refer to the 'enormousness' of the total. This misusage (as in 'the *enormity* of the building') is understandable and is now becoming common. Many people dislike it, so it is better to find another word, such as 'vastness' or 'hugeness'.

enquire or **inquire**

In the UK, these words (unlike **enclose** and **inclose** above) have been moving apart in recent years. To *enquire* or to make an *enquiry* refers more now to asking for information. Because of *Private Eye* perhaps, *inquire* and *inquiry* now relate more to an investigation in some depth. In America, *inquire* and *inquiry* are taking over for both meanings.

What language we habitually speak depends upon a geographical accident. It has nothing to do with the composition of the human sperm or of the human egg.
                    Frederick Bodmer, *The Loom of Language*

ensure or **assure** or **insure**

See **assure**

entrée

In the days when ten-course dinners were standard, an *entrée* (pron: 'ahntray') was a mere aside, served between the fish and meat courses; and it's still used that way on the menus for formal banquets. Grander restaurants may use *Entrées* as the heading for the list of main courses on the menu. But in general now, *entrée* seems to belong to a past world or maybe to the present world of expense-accounts.

envelope

The pronunciation 'ahnvelope' or 'onvelope' is still often heard, as an echo from the time when people felt the word was borrowed from French. Most younger people say 'ennvelope', which is the pronunciation BBC announcers are asked to use.

environment

We no longer believe that the world is a 'bottomless pit' of resources and our fears about how modern societies are polluting the soil, sea and air have taken the word *environment* into the front line of political and social battles. It is used in a 'this planet earth' context but increasingly in a trivial way: 'We live in a nice environment', meaning no more than a pleasant road; and there's the little girl (quoted in Gowers' *Plain Words*) accusing her baby brother, who had wet his pants, of 'polluting his *environment* again'. Because *environment* has become so commonplace, we may now have to talk of 'the physical world around us' to stir people up over the question of industrial and urban wastelands.

> Pollution
> *I shot an*
> *Arrow in the*
> *Sky.*
> *It stuck.*
> Patrick Young (aged 12), *Fire of Spring*

equity

The old 14th-century meaning of justice and fairness remains: 'In all equity' means in all fairness. Much more often now, *equity* is used to mean 'a slice of the action'. If someone asks you to join them in business, they may offer you a share of the *equity* (i.e. shares in the business) instead of a straight salary. Stock markets are called *equity* markets because they sell shares in businesses. (Spelt with a capital, *Equity* is the name of the trade union for actors and actresses.)

erogenous, erotic, erotica, eroticism

Eros, the god of love in Greek mythology, has given birth to some of the more 'respectable' words for our sexual responses. *Erogenous* remains beyond reproach for describing something capable of arousing sexual desire ('*erogenous* zones of the body'). *Eroticism*, also unsullied, is still generally limited to sexual expression in art and literature. But erotic, while remaining in the language of art criticism, has moved down market to take in 'naughty' lingerie and any other cheap pornographic titillation. *Erotica*, once pure Kamasutra (the ancient Sanskrit treatise on love) and used only about esoteric and aesthetic sexual stimulus, is now used about some of the things sold over the counters of sex shops. The cultural use of *erotic* and *erotica*, about a provocative nude by Manet or Picasso's wittily sexy drawings, is still all right, but bear in mind that the same words could well be used down the road to sell a striptease show.

-erous

See **disasterous**

espresso or expresso

This powerful shot-in-the-arm Italian coffee first invaded London in the 1960s, and along with frothy, milky *cappuccino*, has taken over from Surbiton to Stoke-on-Trent. Since the machine sounds like an old steam express train, some people get the name wrong. It is *espresso*, both for the machine and the coffee it makes.

Esq

An *esquire* is 'a member of the English gentry ranking below a knight' (*LD*). It's odd that this bit of gentility, straight out of a Jane Austen novel, should have survived (abbreviated as *Esq*) as a way of addressing a man. It is deservedly dying out in favour of plain 'Mr' or just nothing. Remember: John Brown, *Mr* John Brown (more usual now) or John Brown *Esq* – but never *Mr* John Brown *Esq*.

establishment

This word (usually with a capital: the *Establishment*) has

been used in the last 50 years or so to describe the group of people believed to control our lives and to maintain the existing order. Perhaps it came from the expression 'the Established Church'. The American economist, John Kenneth Galbraith, says: 'The word *Establishment* did not just happen: it gained currency because it describes something.' I agree, although I've never heard anyone say they 'belong to the Establishment', because members of it do not admit that it exists. But it does.

etc. (et cetera)

Even newscasters sometimes slip into saying 'exsetera' instead of 'etsetera'. Some people say we shouldn't use *etc.* at all because it is lazy, yet it is convenient occasionally to avoid giving a long and unnecessary list of things: 'The room was furnished with tables, chairs, bookshelves, etc.' If you don't like *etc.*, you can always use 'and so on'.

euphemisms

In the 21st century more things are out in the open. People no longer 'pass away' – they die. And that long unmentionable disease, cancer, is now spoken about. At the same time, there is a proliferation of *euphemisms*, those gentler or evasive expressions for unpleasant things. Some are worthwhile: 'handicapped' is kinder and less harsh than 'crippled'; and perhaps old-age pensioners prefer to be given the respect of 'senior citizens'. But *euphemisms* can be cover-ups, as when the poor are 'those in lower-income brackets', and 'going into the red' or just plain 'overspending' becomes a 'deficit'. When we believe a linguistic smoke-screen is being put up, we can see what is really going on by changing euphemistic substitutes back into the real words.

Don't call me a senior citizen. Just call me a little old lady.
From a letter to the *New York Times*

Euro or **Euro-** or **euro**

Most *euro* combinations need not be hyphenated, and some can begin with a small *e*: *eurobond* (a bond in euros), *eurocheque*, *eurocurrency*. When the next word begins with a vowel, retain the hyphen: *euro-economics*. Registered names require a capital: Eurostar, Eurotunnel, Eurovision. There's no need to use a capital for the currency: 'We shall pay in euros.' The standard abbreviation is € as in €1000. On the 1st January 2002, euros replaced the national currencies of Austria, Belgium, Eire, Finland, France, Germany, Greece, Italy, Luxembourg, the Netherlands, Portugal and Spain.

everybody

Everybody, like *everyone*, *nobody*, etc. is singular: 'Everybody is ....' By convention, it used to be followed by 'he' or 'his': '*Everybody* should make up *his* own mind.' That is considered by some as sexist. We can wear ourselves out by saying 'his or her' or 'her or his' all the time, or we can use 'their' as a unisex word: '*Everybody* should make up *their* mind.' The grammatical objection is that the plural 'their' conflicts with the singular *everybody*. But language exists for people, not the other way round: 'their' and 'they' are the only convenient unisex words in such sentences and are often used that way. It's not all that new anyway – in the 19th century Thackeray was writing 'Nobody prevents you, do *they*?' See **unisex words**

... despite the fact that a great many well-respected literary figures use they *with* someone *or* anyone, *the current edition of Henry Fowler's* Modern English Usage *still claims that this 'sets the literary man's teeth on edge'. Perhaps a literary woman would be less sensitive!*

Jenny Cheshire, *English Today*

everyone or **every one**
Everyone is for people in general: '*Everyone* turned up.' *Every one* is for things: 'Every one of the glasses was broken.' Use it also for a number of specific people: '*Every one* of the bishops turned up.' See **everybody**

ex
For a long time, *ex* was the easy-going word in the US for a former husband or wife. Now that relationships are less formalized, less permanent and more diverse, *ex* conveniently fills a linguistic gap: it is freely used in America and the UK for a former partner in any relationship, married or not, heterosexual or homosexual. 'My *ex* ...' usually, but not always, implies a friendliness and lack of rancour.

expectant
Nobody says any more that a woman is 'with child'. Fewer people are now saying that she is *expectant*. The word 'pregnant' is back again, although there is no need to say, as they did in the 16th century, that she is 'pregnant with child'.

exquisite
It has been a losing battle to keep the stress on the first syllable ('EXquisite'), and dictionaries now show 'exQUISite' (stress on the second syllable) as an alternative, sometimes even as the preferred pronunciation. But Disgusted of Tunbridge Wells and other die-hards still feel that stress on the second syllable lets the side down. Take whichever side you prefer.

I don't want to talk grammar. I want to talk like a lady ...
Eliza Doolittle, *Pygmalion*

F

face up to

Some purists object to *face up to* as unnecessary because it means the same as 'face'. Yet when we *face up to* something it does suggest a stiffening of resolve, so the phrase is useful. If anyone criticizes it, say it was used as long ago as 1920 by Sir Walter Raleigh, Professor of English at Oxford.

facelift†

Facelift was the word for facial surgery that removed wrinkles and made someone look younger. It has now become extended to include modernizing or cleaning up buildings, statues or almost anything – even a business can be given a *facelift* by bringing in new management. Those discreet clinics in Switzerland no longer perform *facelifts* – now they call it 'cosmetic surgery'.

facile

Although *facile* means easy and without effort, it always carries with it the negative meaning of cheap and superficial. A *facile* argument is one that has not been thought out.

fairy

One of several slang words (in the UK and the US) for a homosexual, that have now almost dropped out of use since homosexual relationships have become more recognized by society. Nowadays *fairies* have gone back to their proper place at the bottom of gardens or on Christmas trees. See **gay, queen, queer**

fall

The American word for 'autumn'. Some of us would like to see this old English word used again in the UK (as it was in the 14th century) as the more poetic and descriptive name for the 'season of mists and mellow fruitfulness'. But there is no sign of this happening.

fall out†

When you *fall out* (two words) with someone you have a row with them. *Fall-out*, with a hyphen, or as one word (*fallout*), is much more sinister because it usually means airborne radioactive debris from a nuclear explosion. Hyphenated or as one word, it is also used now for almost any kind of side-effect, good or bad: *Newsweek* writes about the 'literary fallout' from the war, meaning the books written about it.

fancy

You can *fancy* a drink or you can *'fancy* yourself' (be pleased with the way you look). But to *fancy* a man or a woman ('I rather fancy him') is a slang way of saying you find someone attractive. This was formerly 'working-class' slang but it has become classless and is now used by all ages.

fanny**

This slang word, classed in the UK as 'vulgar', means a woman's genitals, and goes back to 1794, according to one expert on English. That year, a classic on life in a brothel was published, *The Memoirs of Fanny Hill*. The word is still used, often in a friendly way by both men and women. Some years back, the residents of *Fanny Road* in Barnes, London, who couldn't stand the jokes any more, got together and had their road re-named 'St Hilda's Road'. Such is the power of language. In the US, *fanny* is slang (though not considered 'vulgar') for 'backside' and is used for both sexes.

The dictionary-maker has to record what people say, not what he thinks they can politely say ....
Robert Burchfield, former editor
of *Oxford English Dictionaries*

fantasy or **phantasy**

Alternative spellings of the same word. Fantasy is taking over now, probably because of the influence of 'fantastic', and the spelling, *phantasy*, is beginning to look archaic.

fart**

Although treated seriously, as an early English word going back to the 13th century, by Dr C.T. Onions, one of the great 20th-century scholars of the origins of English words, *fart* remains prudishly classified as 'vulgar' by dictionaries.

farther or **further**

There is one difference of use to remember. While a place may be *farther away* or *further away* from somewhere, when it comes to *time* or *something additional*, only *further* should be used: 'until further notice', 'a further payment on account'.

father-in-laws or **fathers-in-law**

See **daughter-in-laws**

fellow-traveller

See **commie**

female

See **woman**

fetish

A word that has two different meanings. To an anthropologist, a *fetish* is an inanimate object worshipped by a primitive tribe. But it is the psychiatrist's use of *fetish* that has become more common: an object or an unexpected part of the body or a piece of clothing that arouses feverish sexual excitement in someone. In Eric Rohmer's film, *Claire's Knee*, a young girl's knee becomes a *fetish*.

fewer or **less**

There is always someone waiting to pounce on you for using these words the wrong way round, usually *less* when it should be *fewer*. Here's how to disappoint them: remember *fewer* is for a *number of things* – *less* for a *quantity*. Bill Bryson, when deputy chief sub-editor of *The Times*, offered a simple rule: use *fewer* when the word after is *plural*; use *less* when it is *singular*: 'There were *fewer* men than women', '*fewer* miles to the gallon', '*less* butter means *fewer* calories', '*less* money means *fewer* goods'. But '*less* than 20 miles away' is more usual than '*fewer* than 20 miles ...' because we take '20 miles' as a 'distance', not separate miles.

fictitious or **fictional**

These are sometimes confused. *Fictitious* means sham or false, a downright lie ('his *fictitious* excuse didn't convince anyone'). *Fictional* describes something that exists only in a novel, or possibly in a play or film, but not in real life.

fiddle

In the 14th century this was already an English word for a stringed instrument played with a bow. But the alternative meaning of *fiddle* has taken such a hold that, in spite of *Fiddler on the Roof*, we now have to say someone 'plays the violin' or is a 'violinist' unless he plays folk music. For even *The Times* uses *fiddle* for almost any kind of crooked deal. By now, the alternative meaning of the word has almost *fiddled* its way into standard English, although no dictionary quite accepts that yet.

fifth

It is easy to drop the second 'f' and say 'fith', but if you care about the way you speak, it's worth making the effort to pronounce it.

finalize

A lot of *-ize* (or -ise) and *-ization* (or -isation) words have invaded English, mostly from America. Even if we don't like them, they are useful shortcuts: 'liquidize', 'pressurize' and even 'hospitalize', etc. Some people have taken a violent turn against *finalize* because they don't like the sound of it and because we already have words such as 'finish' and 'complete'. Others find it useful in the sense of *finalizing* a contract or accounts, where it seems to be a little stronger than 'complete'. In any case, dictionaries now accept *finalize* as undisputed standard English, so the battle is lost or won, depending on which side you're on. See -ise or -ize

finance

There are two ways to say this word and the current 'Oxford' view is that you have the right to choose which one you prefer: 'FINEance' (stress on first syllable) or 'finNANCE' (stress on second syllable).

first or **firstly**

The once hotly debated grammatical rumpus over this has at last fizzled out and no one now seems to mind whether you say *firstly*, *secondly*, *thirdly* ... or *first*, *second*, *third* ..., which seems more in keeping with the language now. Fowler, the most famous English grammarian, considered all along that it was a lot of fuss about nothing.

floor and **ceiling**

See **ceiling**

flu or **'flu†**

Hardly anyone says 'influenza' any more. *Flu* has become the standard word and it is dated now to write *'flu*, any more than we should write *'bus*, *'phone* or *'plane*.

fluke

Used to be associated with a lucky shot in billiards but is now used for *anything* successful that happens by chance rather than through judgement or skill, either in a game or in life. Most people think it is slang or at least informal English. But in fact it is perfectly standard now and

you will read it in a leading article in *The Times* and hear
it used by judges.

focused or **focussed***

The orthodox 'Oxford' preference is *not* to double the
-s-: *focused, focuses, focusing*. The *COD* and *LD* show
-ss- as an alternative, but some editors of books reject it.

foot or **foot-**

Nearly always you can assume that where *foot* combines
with another word, the compound has become one word
and there is no need for a hyphen: football, foothills,
foothold, footlights, footbath, footprint, footstep,
footnote and most of the others. *Foot-brake* and *foot-
bridge* still take a hyphen.

*Other exports may be down but at least the language is
selling well .... English has ousted French as the common
currency of diplomacy, nearly all the information stored in
the world's computers is in English; it is the main language
of commerce, medicine, electronics, and space terminology,
of aviation and navigation at sea.*

Jack Cross in the *Guardian*

for

Whatever anyone says, *'What are you doing it for?'* is
good English. See **prepositions at end of sentences**

forecast or **forecasted**

Was the weather *forecast* or *forecasted*? Both are 'correct'
but *forecast* is so much more usual now, that *forecasted* is
beginning to sound 'wrong'.

forego or **forgo**

The spelling helps us to remember that *forego* is linked
with *before* and that's what it means: to go before ('the
foregoing paragraph'). *Forgo* is a different word and
means to go without: 'He will *forgo* a holiday this year.'

foreign words and **phrases**

Some of these (*per annum, ad infinitum, hors d'oeuvre, et
cetera*) have made their home in English and hardly seem
foreign any more. Many more, such as restaurant, hotel,
rapport, have become English. There are others which
are borderline or not readily understood by most people.
If we use these, it can sound affected or like showing off,

which it often is. But the purpose of language, as G.M. Young said, 'is to get an idea as exactly as possible out of one mind into another', and if a foreign word or phrase says it for you in the way that no English expression can, why not use it, *provided* you know the other person will understand? There is, after all, such a thing as *le mot juste*.

for ever or **forever**

Some people make a subtle and perhaps unnecessary distinction between *for ever*, meaning for all time ('I will love you *for ever*') and *forever* meaning persistently ('He's *forever* saying that'). In America, *forever* is always one word and this is now becoming usual in the UK, although it used to be objected to.

form

We can still be in *good form* when we're playing tennis (or performing well at any other activity) or we can be *in good form*, when we're feeling well. We can just about still ask *What's the form?* meaning how do you go about things here, although it does sound dated. But be careful now about saying something is *bad form* as it could make you sound like a Colonel Blimp.

format†

Once restricted to typography and printing, *format* is now used for the arrangement or layout of almost anything: 'the *format* of a TV show', 'the *format* of a sales conference'. In computer language, *format* is the arrangement of data for processing or storage.

formulae or **formulas**

Mathematicians or scientists would say *formulae* (pron: 'FORmulee') for more than one *formula*; at least some of the older ones would. Nearly everybody else now says *formulas*, the normal English plural of the word.

fortuitous

Something that happens by chance, with the implication that it was a lucky chance: 'His *fortuitous* arrival saved the situation.' Because it sounds a little like 'fortunate', it is often wrongly given the same meaning: 'In the end the delay turned out to be *fortuitous*.' The right word there is 'fortunate'. But this misusage has become so common that not many people notice it any more.

four-letter words

These are the words that might make our maiden aunts
and a lot of other people blush, or produce a stony silence.
For many years rigorously excluded from dictionaries,
newspapers and books, the door was at last opened to
them in 1960, when Penguin Books published the full version of D.H. Lawrence's *Lady Chatterley's Lover*. They
were brought to trial at the Old Bailey in London, eminent
literary critics gave evidence for them, and Penguin Books
won the case. That heralded the 'swinging '60s', a more
open freedom to explore human experience and the linguistic reverberations from all that. Yet more than 20 years
later, the 1982 *COD* stated magisterially that four-letter
words are 'used only by those who have no wish to be
thought either polite or educated'. That's a slap in the face
for the BBC, a number of leading novelists on both sides
of the Atlantic (including at least one Nobel Prizewinner
for Literature), many critics and journalists, good poets
such as Philip Larkin, me and perhaps you too.

Eric Partridge, a respected lexicographer, considered
that some of these words 'belong to the aristocracy of the
language'. Dr C.T. Onions, one of the editors of the great
Oxford English Dictionary, includes many of the words in
his major dictionary of English etymology. Gerald Long,
at the time managing director of Times Newspapers,
cheerfully used 'turd' and 'shit' in a talk for the BBC; similar words in *English Observed*, a book by Philip Howard,
literary editor of *The Times* at the time, were included in
extracts specially chosen by the BBC.

After all that, where do the rest of us stand? What is
obscene in language is defined by law as tending to
'deprave and corrupt persons who are likely, having
regard to all relevant circumstances, to read ... it'. But
what is *vulgar* or *indecent* is 'all in the mind', dependent
on social convention, different at different times and
among different groups.

We now have to decide for ourselves whether to toe
the linguistic line, which is not all that clearly defined
now anyway, or to use the language that belongs to us in
ways that are natural to us and *appropriate* to the situation. For as Randolph Quirk (when Professor of English

at London University) put it: 'There is nothing liberal or *liberated* in getting a thrill out of linguistic flashing at old ladies ....' At the same time, the words are there – and have been for centuries – waiting to be used whenever 'polite' evasions would be pussyfoot hypocrisy.

We must take the roughnecks with the smoothies and accept that any major social movement will spawn its deviants. Taken as a whole, I remain convinced that the sociolinguistic health of English speakers now is in better shape than when Dickens could congratulate himself on avoiding speech that might 'offend the ear'.
Randolph Quirk, *The State of the Language*

Fowler

When you discuss English with some people, they say 'But *Fowler* says ....' Fowler's *Modern English Usage*, his most famous book, is a classic, as much as anything for its cool urbane style, and it does not diminish it to say that, like the rest of us, he had personal prejudices and quirks about the use of English. *Henry Watson Fowler* died in 1933 (his book has been re-edited since) and his linguistic edicts are not Holy Writ, true for all times. 'Our time is a time for crossing barriers,' said Marshall McLuhan, in a later pronouncement on language, 'for erasing old categories – for probing ground.' English is keeping pace with that.

I think the only reason languages disappear is when they lose any creative power.
Isaac Bashevis Singer, Nobel Prizewinner
for Literature (1978)

foyer

When you meet someone in the *foyer* of a theatre or a hotel in the UK, you can pronounce it either 'foy-ay' or the French way, 'fwah-yay'. Both are 'correct'. In America they prefer to say it as it is spelt: 'foy-er'.

fracas

Keep your cool if you get mixed up in a *fracas* (a noisy row) and remember to pronounce it 'frack-ah' (but 'fraykus' in America).

81

freight or goods
See **goods**

fresh

BBC newscasters are advised against talking about '*fresh* fighting breaking out' or '*fresh* talks taking place', and to use the word 'new' instead. But *fresh* is used frequently that way, in the news and in conversation ('Here's some *fresh* information'), because many people find this a lively and effective use of the word.

Freudian slip†

The Austrian psychologist, Sigmund Freud, put the unconscious on the map. We saw that below the surface of our apparent attitudes and behaviour, there is another personality, usually concealed from others. A *Freudian slip* is when we accidentally say something that seems to be a mistake, but in fact reveals some aspect of our unconscious.

fringe

Perhaps it all started with *Beyond the Fringe*, a successful comedy show of the 1960s that launched Jonathan Miller and others. Now there's no end to the usefulness of *fringe* to describe something outside or additional to what is standard: *fringe benefits*, *fringe theatre*, *fringe medicine* – and I've even heard *fringe sex*, although I'm not quite sure what *that* means.

frisson

You cannot have a 'slight frisson' or a 'great frisson', both of which I've seen in print. *Frisson* is always light-weight because in French it means a shiver or a shudder. So a *frisson* is a tremor of nervous excitement that someone or a group of people experience. Sometimes it is printed in italics as a foreign word but often now it is accepted as normal English, although still pronounced as in French 'FREESsonn'.

fuck***

Once the most notorious of all the 'four-letter words', *fuck* is used so often now, in speech and in print, that it might become almost acceptable eventually. But that has not happened yet. The critic, Kenneth Tynan, was the first person to utter the word on the BBC when, on 13 November 1965, presumably unrehearsed and certainly unscripted, he said *fuck* on a TV programme.

Consternation and panic followed. Now it is heard often in TV and radio plays, interviews and readings from books. It is printed in the *Observer*, on the women's page of the *Guardian*, used in serious poetry published by respected publishers, and given full frontal exposure in dictionaries. The literal meaning of *fuck* is, of course, to copulate, and for some women and men it is preferable in that sense to the vague 'make love' or the clinical 'have sex'. *Fuck* can still cause serious offence so if you use it, be prepared for the shock waves. See **four-letter words**

funny

When someone asks 'Do you mean funny-peculiar or funny-*ha-ha*?' it is because dictionaries accept that the word has these two meanings. A *funny* situation can be a joke or it can be a situation that is tricky and delicate. Where there's a doubt, it is better to make sure you say what you mean.

furore

A *furore* (meaning an uproar) in the UK has three syllables: 'fewRAWry'. The same commotion in America would have only two syllables: 'FEWraw'.

G

gaffe
Used to mean a social blunder, like eating peas off a knife, but is now used in standard English for almost any kind of blush-making mistake. Don't confuse it with 'gaff', which has all kinds of other meanings, the most common being a spar to which a mainsail is attached.

Gallup poll
It should mean a sounding of public opinion carried out by one of the companies founded by Dr Horace Gallup. He is the American who more or less invented the statistical method, using a so-called 'representative sample' of the population, for assessing public attitudes about anything from a detergent to voting intention in elections. A *Gallup poll* is sometimes used loosely for any public-opinion poll, whether or not carried out by the Gallup organization.

gambit
The extended use of this word has become general,

and as so often happens, it is now more common than the original meaning, which was an opening move in chess where you sacrifice a pawn or piece to secure an advantage. Now a calculated move in *any* situation, that makes things go your way, is called a clever or shrewd *gambit*. An *opening gambit* (although you could argue that *opening* is unnecessary since *gambit* is an opening move anyway) is used for a clever opening remark.

garage
In the UK always stress the *first* syllable, even if you slip into the pronunciation 'GAridge', as so many people do now. In America, stress the *second* syllable: 'gaRAHGE'.

Certain things drive me bananas. When, for example, announcers say 'excetera' for etcetera or 'garridge' for garage, I get someone to mention it to them. Why should we teach half London to pronounce words wrongly?

John Whitney, when managing
director of Capital Radio

gas

Though you can *step on the gas* and even *run out of gas* in the UK, *gas* has never become the usual word for 'petrol', as it is in America, where gas is an abbreviation of 'gasoline'.

gay

If you say 'I feel gay' or 'You look gay', meaning lively or carefree or dressed in bright colours, you are likely to get a laugh or a snigger, although those remain the primary meanings of gay in dictionaries. With the help of the *Gay Liberation* movement and *Gay News* (weekly magazine started in 1972) *gay* now means, more than anything else, homosexual. It has taken over from expressions such as 'queer', 'queen' and the desperately dated 'pansy'. Sadly, the former meanings of *gay* have been superseded. That is not prejudice, by the way, just regret at losing a happy and useful word.

> *It was a good word once, a little sparkler,*
> *Simple, innocent even, like a hedgerow flower …*
> *A good word once, and I'm disconsolate*
> *And angered by this simple syllable's fate:*
> *A small innocence gone, a little Fall.*
> *I grieve the loss. I am not gay at all.*
> > Vernon Scannell, from *Protest Poem*,
> > published in the *New Statesman*

gazump

How did we ever manage without this word, which is another one of those colourful enrichments of English from Yiddish? It is still used mostly in connection with buying and selling property. In case you have never been gazumped, it means raising the price after accepting an offer and before the deal is legalized.

gearing†

With gears, a large cogged wheel drives a smaller one at a faster speed. *Gearing* is a financial application of that principle. When you invest money on the understanding that you pay only a small percentage of the sum to begin with and the rest later on, that is *gearing*: a small sum is doing the work of a larger sum. If the investment goes up in value before you need to pay the full sum, you can sell and make a killing. But gearing is not surefire: if the investment goes down in value and you do not have the funds to pay the balance when the time comes, you are in trouble.

generalissimo†

A colourful Italian word, part of standard English, for the supreme commander of different armies working together or of a combined army, navy and air force. It is a word occasionally used now for the person of either sex who is running any big show, such as one of the multi-national companies. Pron: 'generalLISSsimo'.

genius

There is a tendency to dilute the special quality of this word for describing someone with truly exalted powers as an artist, scientist or thinker. *Genius* doubles more and more these days for mere aptitude or talent: 'She has a genius for making soufflés.' If we use it *that* way, what word do we have left for Mozart or Einstein?

gentleman

In these egalitarian times, *gentleman* is becoming a rather quaint word, and a secretary is not so likely to say 'There's a *gentleman* to see you.' But after-dinner speakers keep the word alive: 'Ladies and *gentlemen* ....' So do

MPs, even if they don't mean it: 'The honourable *gentle-man* ....'

genuine

Genuine rhymes with 'feminine'. It does not usually rhyme with 'swine', although we hear that pronunciation sometimes, especially in Ireland.

gimmick

Television and the other media are greedy for new words and *gimmick*, already current in the US in the 1920s and which rocketed to fame in the UK in the 1950s, is becoming dated. Yet it will stay with us, because it's so useful, in our world of cheap publicity tricks, to describe something that has no real purpose except to get attention.

gipsy or **gypsy**

Dictionaries accept both as 'correct' but since the name is connected with 'Egypt', where gypsies were supposed to have originated, *gypsy* is preferable. When the people or their language are meant, *Gypsy*, with a capital 'G', is appropriate, but not when we're using gypsy to describe something ('a *gypsy* way of life').

girl

Feminists consider that this simple innocent word is the most sexist of all. Here are some one-time definitions of *girl* in the *COD*: '... woman working in office, shop, factory, etc., woman secretary or other assistant ...'. Feminists argue that we would not call a man over 18 a *boy*, so why call a grown woman a *girl*, with its belittling implication of immaturity and lack of importance? They believe that deep-seated attitudes will change only when we consciously change words that reflect them. Other women find all this exaggerated. It is certainly a long-established habit, for both sexes, to talk about women as 'girls', although we should be aware that some women object to this very strongly. You still hear *old girl* used affectionately by some men to their wives or women friends, although it does sound like yesterday's language. *Girlie* is the most offensive of all as it is so often used about porn magazines and photographs. See **sexist words**

Is there really a built-in masculine bias in English, that we need to be constantly on our guard against? And if there is, does it matter? Or is it simply that the language reflects a traditional cultural bias? If so, it seems very likely that, as the social roles of men and women change, so the English language will change, to keep pace with the changes in our cultural outlook.

Jenny Cheshire, *English Today*

girlfriend

Used in the UK, and even more in America, by one woman about another, and usually carries no hint of a sexual relationship between them. See **boyfriend**

given name

In America, any of one's names other than the surname. It has never caught on in the UK, where 'Christian name', used on official forms for many years, has been replaced by 'first name'.

glamorous

Roundly trounced in the early 1970s by the lexicographer, Eric Partridge, as 'the dubious privilege of boss-driven copywriters', *glamorous* has become respectable English, even if used rather loosely sometimes. If it appeals to you, use it about an occasion, a love-affair, a person (usually a

woman) or anything else that has enchantment and magic. In America, the 'u' drops out (as is usual with British -*our* words) and *glamour* becomes 'glamor'. But 'glamourous'** is wrong everywhere.

glossies

Imported from the US in the 1950s, the word *glossies* (nearly always used in the plural) is now accepted by some dictionaries as standard English. It is certainly a useful word to describe those showy shiny expensive-looking magazines.

gobbledygook

A word, said to have been invented by President Roosevelt, that has become standard English in the UK as well as the US. It deserved to, because it's such an expressive word to attack academic, political or official writing and speaking, that is submerged into incomprehensibility by the sheer weight of polysyllables. In case *that* sounds like *gobbledygook* to anyone, what I mean is – 'using too many long words'.

God or god

God always takes a capital in the Christian religion. Also in such expressions as *Thank God!*, *For God's sake* .... In everyday use, it's a small *g*: 'Money is his god', 'She treats him like a god.'

goods or freight

In America *freight* covers merchandise transported by train, road, sea or air. In the UK, the custom (but not a strict rule) is to use *goods* when they are transported by land, and *freight* when transported by sea or air. But it's not uncommon to hear *freight* train in the UK as well.

got

Some people think the word is ugly. It is sometimes unnecessary, but that does not make it 'wrong', which is also claimed. Shakespeare, Swift, Ruskin and Dr Johnson all used it. 'I haven't *got* it in stock' is down to earth. 'I don't have it in stock' is more formal. With that difference in mind, use *got* whenever it suits you. In America, 'I haven't got' would be rare as it's usually 'I don't have'; they also retain 'gotten' ('I have gotten it for you'), which used to be British usage too but no longer, except in 'ill-gotten gains'.

gourmand or **gourmet**

A *gourmand* eats like a pig; a *gourmet* eats with discrimination and refinement. Pron: 'GOORmahn' and
'GOORmay'.

goy

What is this Yiddish word, meaning a *Gentile*, doing in a
book about good English – already? The word has to
some extent 'passed' and you even occasionally hear non-
Jews using it about themselves in a good-humoured way.
For some Jews, *goy* is no longer derogatory as it used to
be, and they might use it warmly to and about their non-
Jewish friends. Any linguistic change that diminishes
racism is good news, which is why *goy* has a place in this
book. See **Yinglish**

graffiti

These are usually what Randolph Quirk calls 'spray-gun
obscenities flagrantly unignorable on walls in Chicago or
London'. But *graffiti* are not always obscene; they can be
political or funny. Although *graffiti* is standard English
now, the word is as Italian as spaghetti, and is *plural* ('The
graffiti *are* …'). The singular 'graffito' is not usually used
in English, except by people trying to show off their
Italian. Pron: 'graFEEtee'.

gramophone

If you listen to records on a machine with a large horn
emerging from it, you can still call it a *gramophone*.
Otherwise, the collective term *hi-fi* or *stereo* is now used.

gray or **grey**

Not so long ago, these were alternatives, but now *gray**
seems affected, except in the US where it is the normal
spelling.

grievious or **grievous**

Perhaps because of 'devious', some people get this wrong.
Grievous is right.

grisly or **grizzly**

Both words sound the same, so they're easily mixed up.
Grisly means gruesome and ghastly ('a grisly apparition').
Grizzly is simply grey-haired, now used more about *bears*
than people.

ground zero

This sinister expression from the mid-20th century has
unexpectedly been given an even more sinister meaning
early on in the 21st century. *Ground zero* was first used in
the *New York Times* in 1946 for the devastation directly
below a nuclear explosion. When the twin towers of the
World Trade Center were brought down by the terrorist
attack on September 11th 2001, the vast cataclysmic area
of rubble became known officially as *Ground Zero*. The
name will be with New Yorkers for years to come, perhaps forever.

guarantee or **guaranty**

Some people preserve a distinction between these two
words, using *guaranty* for the piece of paper you are
given that *guarantees* something. It has become more
usual to use *guarantee* for *all* meanings of the word.

guerilla

A word often in the news yet many people are uncertain
about it. It's a word from the Spanish Civil War; *guerilla*
fighting is harassment of established forces by small independent groups. The fighters in those groups are
guerillas. Spelling is either *guerilla* or *guerrilla* and it
often sounds the same as 'gorilla', which is awkward. To
make it sound different, give the 'e' the *unstressed* 'e'
sound of 'get': 'gehRILla'. Look out for verbal tricks with
this word. When people are against them, *guerillas* may
be used in the same way as 'terrorists'. But when they are
considered useful, they may be called 'freedom fighters'.
See **psycholinguistics**

guesstimate

An invented word that makes some people wince. But it tells you where you stand: the figure quoted is so rough that it's only one step up from a guess. In fact, when you see the final bill, many 'estimates' turn out to have been guesstimates anyway. Spell it with a *double-s* (although guestimate is an accepted alternative), to make it look more like a guess than a real estimate.

guru

This Sanskrit word travelled to the West in the 1960s. The Beatles and others, satiated with the pleasures of materialism, looked to *gurus* in India for another meaning in life. In Hinduism, a *guru* is a personal spiritual teacher and guide. Since then, alas, the West has corrupted the word. *Guru* is now used for the leader of any new cult or system: I've read of 'the *guru* of modern marketing concepts', which is light-years away from spiritual enlightenment.

guy

This warm conversational word for 'a fellow' is classless. You hear it at all levels of society, especially in the US, but also in the UK. For Damon Runyon (who wrote *Guys and Dolls*) guy became underworld poetry. If it comes naturally to you, why not say someone's a nice guy or you're meeting a guy for dinner? After all, *guy* is said to derive from *Guy Fawkes*, who was British enough.

H

hallucinogenic†

Not as fashionable a word as it was in the 1960s when Timothy Leary, a former faculty member of Harvard, started a cult in the US to promote a shortcut to spiritual enlightenment through the use of LSD and mescaline. These are hallucinogenic drugs – they induce hallucinations and visions. Pron: 'haLUCEsinoGENic'.

hanged or **hung**

You *hang* a picture or wallpaper or *hang* your coat up; an executioner can *hang* a person. If it happened yesterday, the picture, etc. were *hung* but the person was *hanged*.

hangover

The *COD* has moved *hangover* up from 'slang' to standard English, so it's sanctioned for use in formal writing. About time too, because what other word is there to describe that unspeakable morning-after feeling? *Hangover* is extended to cover anything from the past that hasn't altogether disappeared.

hara-kiri

With Japanese films being shown in the West, this word has come into our orbit, and is often misspelt and mispronounced 'hari-kari'. It is ritual suicide by a samurai when faced with defeat or disgrace. Pron: 'harra-KIRri'.

harassment

Harassment has taken on social meanings. *Police harassment* describes unwarranted interference by the police in people's lives. *Union harassment* refers to disruptive activities of trade unions. For women, *harassment* now has first and foremost a sexist meaning: men deliberately brushing up against them or making suggestive remarks. This is *sexual harassment* which has become a bisexual term, since it is not unknown for a woman to inflict it on a man. In the UK, stress *first* syllable: 'HARassment'; in America, *second*: 'haRASSment' (often heard in the UK as well and criticized by some people).

hardly

People sometimes forget that *hardly* is already *negative*, and that a second negative should not be added: 'Without hardly a sound, he left', 'I couldn't hardly hear him',

'Hardly no one understood.'** Those should be: 'With hardly a sound …', 'I could hardly …', 'Hardly anyone ….' The same goes for *scarcely*.

hardware

The first meaning that may now come to mind is for the electronic equipment of computers. *Military hardware* covers guns, tanks and so on. It is too soon to say whether the old meaning will eventually fade out altogether but in the meantime, remember that *hardware* shops do not sell computers or tanks.

haven't

See **contracted forms**

haves and **have-nots**†

Not exactly the same as 'the rich and the poor', as it used to be. *Haves* are not necessarily rich – they may simply have a job.

he or **she**

Leases and other legal documents still often say 'words importing the masculine gender shall be deemed to include females' or some other expression of male smugness. For centuries, *he* in certain situations was taken to include *she*. The 1975 Sex Discrimination Act and the feminist movement have made us less comfortable about that. If we use *he or she* to deal with this problem, perhaps we should keep the balance by occasionally using *she or he*. You or your readers will soon get tired of that, so for another solution, see **everybody**.

… it begins to seem a good idea to vary word order and to let women have a turn at coming first – perhaps particularly now that the hypocritical habit of letting them pass through the doorways first seems to be disappearing!

Jenny Cheshire, *English Today*

headmaster and **headmistress**

More and more words are being replaced by words that do not specify whether it's a woman or a man. While *headteacher* is not the standard word yet, it is seen and heard all the time.

heaven

When *heaven* is a synonym for God, use a capital: 'for *Heaven's* sake', 'in *Heaven's* name', but not otherwise.

Hebrew and **Yiddish**

I was surprised recently when someone told me they believed *Yiddish* to be a conversational form of *Hebrew*, and Eric Partridge, in *Usage and Abusage*, says this is a common misconception. It may be because writers in *Yiddish*, such as Isaac Bashevis Singer, the Nobel Prizewinner, use the *Hebrew* alphabet. The two languages are completely different from each other. *Hebrew*, like Arabic, is a Semitic language, and was adopted as the national language of the State of Israel. *Yiddish* is European, a dialect derived from German with words from other languages (including Hebrew), and spoken by Jews in or from Central and Eastern Europe. See **Yinglish**

here- words

Herein, hereof, hereto, hereunder, herewith and so on appear much less frequently than they used to in business letters and letters from government departments. I *hereby* declare that they are pompous legalese and should be avoided whenever possible.

hero and **heroine**

While *heroine* is the more usual word for a woman, *hero* has joined the list of unisex words and it is all right to use it now, as accepted by recent dictionaries, about a woman as well as a man. Plural: *heroes*.

hers or **her's**

Her's is *always* wrong.

highbrow

Although still used about someone who glories in being intellectual, it is being replaced by 'egghead', which is more derogatory. This reflects the growing distrust of anyone who functions only with the intellect. See **academic**

high-powered

There is less certainty today that driving activity is altogether admirable. When *high-powered* is used about a woman or a man, to mean thrusting and dynamic, it may also now carry with it the hint of blind ruthless ambition.

high street or **main street**

At one time, *high street* in the UK equalled *main street* in the US. But *main street* is now heard frequently in Britain as well ('Where's the *main street*?'). Use either, except, of course, where *High Street* is the actual name of the road.

hijack or **highjack**

Hijack.

Hindi or **Hindu** or **Hindustani**

Westerners get confused about which is which. *Hindi* is the name of one of the official languages of Northern India. It is also a literary language with much of the vocabulary derived from Sanskrit. After the establishment of the Indian Republic, *Hindi* was selected as the *lingua franca* of India. *Hindustani*, an earlier name for *Hindi*, is rarely used these days. A Hindu is a person who is a follower of the spiritual and social creeds of Hinduism, which embrace a belief in reincarnation. At one time, *Hindu* was used loosely to mean any inhabitant of the Indian sub-continent but that usage would be altogether out of place now***.

historic or **historical**

Something that *makes* history is *historic*: 'That was a historic event.' Something that *describes* or *belongs* to history is *historical*: 'Here's a *historical* account of the event.' 'For *historic* reasons', commonly heard, should be 'for *historical* reasons' (for reasons related to history). But note that the financial world refers to *historic costs* and *historic rates of interest* and although that is 'wrong', it is accepted – for *historical* reasons.

hoard or **horde**

They both *sound* the same so when we come to write them, we may hesitate. *Hoard* is to accumulate things or the accumulation itself – a miser *hoards* money and his money is a *hoard*. *Horde*, no longer a rare word used about nomadic tribes, means a disorderly crowd: 'a *horde* of football hooligans'.

holocaust

A *holocaust* can mean the wholesale slaughter of people and is sometimes also used for great loss of life by accident. With a capital 'H' (*Holocaust*), it is the name given to the persecution and murder of millions of Jews by Nazi Germany.

homoeopathy

Fringe medicine is in fashion and *homoeopathy* is the practice of giving the patient minute doses of remedies that induce a mild form of the disease they are intended to cure. This activates the natural healing powers of the body. The practitioners, often qualified doctors, are *homoeopaths*. The spelling is tricky unless you remember that *homo* is from a Greek word meaning *same*. Pron: 'homeeOPpathy' and 'HOMEmiapath'.

homosexual

It is often felt that this covers sexual relations only between *men*. The word does not come from Latin *homo* meaning 'man' (*homo sapiens*) but from Greek *homos*, meaning 'same'. *Homosexual* can refer to women as well as men. The famous Wolfenden Report, finally adopted by Parliament in 1967, recommended legalizing *male* homosexuality, since female homosexuality was not illegal. The misunderstanding is so widespread that it is better to go along with it and use *homosexual* only about men, keeping *lesbian* for women. Pronunciation is another problem: we are recommended to preserve the link with Greek and say 'hommosexual', not 'home-o-sexual'. Dictionaries accept both, and most people prefer 'home-o-sexual' or *homo* (pronounced 'home-o'). See **gay**

hopefully

This has become the Great Linguistic Bore of our time. Some people foam at the mouth over what they declare angrily is the wrong use of *hopefully*, 'the final descent into darkness for the English language', as someone has written. What a fuss! The accepted meaning is 'full of hope': 'He set off hopefully' or, as in Robert Louis Stevenson's famous line: 'To travel hopefully is a better thing than to arrive.' The other use is to say 'it is hoped': '*Hopefully* business will pick up.' There is a technical grammatical objection to this, but 'happily', 'regrettably', 'apparently' and several other words (even 'more importantly') are all used in the same way and no one minds: 'Happily they were able to agree.' Because it's useful, the alternative use of *hopefully* has gained so much ground that people who hated it at one time find themselves using it this way. A few can still get quite violent about it. When you use *hopefully* to mean 'it is hoped', there are a lot of people on your side, but be prepared for someone to shout at you. *Hopefully*, this will be the last word on the subject.

The language is in rude health, so long as we can go on using it, abusing it, complaining about it, and changing it in so many rich and varied ways.

Philip Howard, *Words Fail Me*

horrible, horribly

These were strong words once and perhaps we should resist taking the guts out of them by using them in trivial ways: 'It was a *horrible* meal', 'You're *horribly* late.' And how about *horror-comics* for a contradiction in terms?

hors d'oeuvres

Grander and even some more modest restaurants still put this on the menu, as part of classic gastronomic vocabulary, but most other places have switched to 'starters'.

hospitable

Although it comes naturally to some people to put the

stress on the *second* syllable ('hosPITable'), it is more up-market to stress the first: 'HOSpitable'.

hospitalize

One of the post-war **-ise** or **-ize** words that many of us, including me, dislike. It is accepted by most current dictionaries as a standard way of saying 'admit to hospital'.

host

To *host* a dinner-party, meaning 'to be the host at', is not a usage that all of us find comfortable, except about TV programmes ('to *host* a chat-show'). But the distinguished civil servant, Sir Bruce Fraser, in *Plain Words*, finds it 'a useful and respectable recruit to the language'. With such an endorsement, perhaps we should all feel free to use *host* in this way. Current dictionaries also accept the usage.

hotel

A few people still drop the 'h' and say *'otel*, as was more usual earlier this century. A hangover from that is to say *an* hotel, rather than *a* hotel. While neither *'otel* nor *an hotel* are 'wrong', they are both obsolete. See **a** or **an**

housewife

It was usual at one time for many women to give their occupation as *housewife*. For some the word now has an uneasy ring to it. Some women prefer *wife and mother*, others are not sure. Established social ideas have changed and in some cases, English has not always caught up. No one, except possibly elderly recluses, uses the old pronunciation 'hussif'.

... we persist in talking about a 20th-century problem in an outmoded 17th-century vocabulary.
John Searle, as Professor of Philosophy,
Berkeley University

humankind
A unisex word that is not yet readily accepted, although it seems a good way of avoiding unnecessary masculine bias in English. This doesn't mean we should lose our heads and call holes in the road – 'humanholes'!

hype
Hyperbole is admittedly rather a literary word, so *hype* has become a convenient slang abbreviation for it, meaning extravagant and probably exaggerated praise for something: 'show-biz hype', 'media hype'.

Slang is the language of the future.
Robert Burchfield, BBC Radio 4

hyphens

The style-book of the Oxford University Press, New York, is quoted as saying 'If you take *hyphens* seriously you will surely go mad.' Now you've been warned, let's continue. The tendency is to *drop* the hyphen when a newly combined word becomes familiar: air-strip – airstrip, space-suit – spacesuit, ice-cream – icecream. But sometimes it gets stuck: bus-stop, coffee-pot (although teapot). It helps to use a hyphen in combined numbers from twenty-one to ninety-nine. At other times, a hyphen can make something clear: 'The woman has ten inch long feet' might produce a double-take which a couple of hyphens could prevent – 'ten-inch-long feet'. Use hyphens to help the people who will read what you are writing, and if a hyphen looks right to the eye, that's almost as good a guide as any. To take it further, read the six tightly packed columns of advice in the original edition of Fowler's *Modern English Usage*, but remember the warning at the beginning of this entry. See **co** or **co-** and **re** or **re-**

I

I or me

Grammatical terms, such as 'subjective' and 'accusative', are useful for explaining things, but not everyone is familiar with them. They can also put language into a strait-jacket and generally I have avoided using such terms in this book. Even if you're not sure why, please take on trust that 'between you and me', 'for you and me', 'after you and me' and many similar phrases are perfect English. Yet some educated people lapse happily into the false grammar of 'between you and I', 'for you and I', etc. So 'upper-class' is this error, that *between you and I* has been called the nob's phrase. Even Shakespeare wrote 'All debts are cleared between you and I'; Pepys contributed 'Wagers lost between him and I', and Dickens chipped in with 'Leave Nell and I to toil and work.' On TV, David Dimbleby gave us 'From you and I', and Angela Rippon 'from Arthur Negus and I'. I hope I shall go to the grave saying 'between you and me'. Nevertheless, Robert Burchfield, when chief editor of *Oxford English Dictionaries*, reluctantly admitted that the nob's ungrammatical 'between you and I' is 'racing away into general, even educated use'. And it really is, as Brian Foster points out, the *Queen's English*, quoting Her Majesty saying on her return from a Commonwealth tour: 'It's a wonderful moment for my husband and I.' See **myself**

The legend that Ross [editor of the New Yorker*] put a comma in 'I saw her but a moment' because of the danger that the reader might misconstrue the fourth word is not true. Love to you and she from Helen and I.*

James Thurber, in a letter to Lewis Gannett
at the *New York Herald Tribune*

-ible or -able
See **-able**
i.e. or e.g.
See **e.g.**

if I was or if I were

This involves the 'subjunctive', a grammatical subtlety difficult for most people to understand and not altogether at home in English anyway. When the subjunctive is used, it can sound formal and stuffy: 'I am concerned that the truth *be* known', rather than the more natural '... is known'. Even if you do not want to go into the whole business further, it is worth noting that even the *one* use of the subjunctive that was generally considered good educated usage: 'If I were' and 'if he, she or it were' is giving way to 'If I was', etc.

English grammar is a complicated system never quite mastered even by the best speakers of English.

Robert Burchfield, *The Spoken Word*

illegitimate

See **bastard**

illusion or delusion

See **delusion**

image

'We must do something about our *image*.' When the head of a company or of a political party says that, they do not mean they must be more honest, do a better job, offer better value, but that they must look as if they are doing those things. It is the job of advertising and public relations to 'create' an image, which need have nothing to do with the truth but is good for business, getting votes or whatever. The great importance of *image* in the 21st century is a sinister admission of hypocrisy and the manipulation of opinion. See **brainwashing**

Don't tell my mother I'm in Advertising ... she thinks I play the piano in a brothel

Title of a book by Jacques Séguéla, head of a successful Paris ad agency

imbalance†

A medical and physiological term ('a hormonal imbalance') that has developed wider applications. An *imbalance* in our income could mean we spend half our time earning only one tenth of our income. An *imbalance* of trade is a lack of balance between sections of a country's economy.

immanent or **imminent**

Both are pronounced in almost the same way and are occasionally mixed up. *Immanent* is something naturally within us, an undeniable inner force: 'Sexual drive is *immanent* throughout nature.' *Imminent* is something threatening that is about to happen: 'He is in *imminent* danger of getting the sack.'

immoral or **amoral**

See **amoral**

impasse

Both the French and English pronunciation are all right: 'AMpass' or 'IMpass'.

imply or **infer**

A speaker or a writer *implies* when they suggest or hint at something. When we read or listen, we *infer*, that is we 'read between the lines' and pick up what was really intended. Be on guard against using *infer* when you mean *imply*: 'Do you *infer* that I am wrong?' should be 'Do you *imply* ....' Remember that someone *implies* what someone else *infers*.

important or **importantly**

More importantly is trendy and gives some people a nice sense of self-importance, so they prefer it to *more important*, especially when speaking in public or on TV. There are grammatical arguments both ways. William Safire, who was Richard Nixon's speech-writer, gives this advice: '*More important* is my preference, but if *more importantly* turns you on, go ahead and use it.' That's where I stand too.

impractical or **impracticable**

There's an important distinction. If you are no good at doing the everyday things in life, you are *impractical*; if something isn't worth doing because, for example, it's too complicated or not worth the expense, that is also impractical. If something is *impracticable* it means it simply would not work or is an idea that could not possibly be carried out.

impresario or impressario

Impressario may look right but it is wrong. The word is *impresario*.

in

Whatever anyone says, '*What did you put it in?*' is good English. See **prepositions at end of sentences**

in- or un-

I'm sorry but there is no reliable rule to tell you whether it is indetectable or undetectable, inexperienced or unexperienced and so on (*undetectable* and *inexperienced* are right, by the way). If you want to be sure, turn to a dictionary.

incidentally or incidently

A whole string of syllables is awkward to say which is why *incidently* is often heard and creeps into writing as well. Say and write *incidentally*.

inclose or enclose

See **enclose**

incomparable

Stress the *second* syllable rather than the *third*: 'inCOMparable'.

index

Since inflation may always be with us, we have to learn the new application of *index*, as in *Retail Price Index*, the series of related prices showing the rise in the cost of living. Wages, pensions, investments or anything else are *indexed* when they are automatically adjusted to take into account a rise or fall in prices. They are then *index-linked*. *Indexation*, a recent word for index-linking, is the only way to guarantee the purchasing power of money. The standard plural of *index* is now *indexes* (only in scientific applications is *indices* still sometimes used).

industrial action

This vague expression, beloved by trade unions and the media, covers anything from bashing the boss to striking, banning overtime or going to work five minutes late.

industrialist

There's no need to be impressed if someone calls themselves an *industrialist*, since it covers anyone making anything from tin cans to tanks. See **capitalist**

inedible or **uneatable**
　　See **eatable**
infectious or **contagious**
　　See **contagious**
infer or **imply**
　　See **imply**
inflation

We all know, literally to our cost, what *inflation* means, and we have to learn the new words connected with it, if we are to understand MPs and the media. *Hyperinflation* means a runaway rate of inflation. *Deflation* means prices going down. *Disinflation* is a smoke-screen word because it means that prices are still going up but not as fast. Lastly, *stagflation* is almost the worst of all, because it means that prices are rising while industrial output remains stagnant.

infrastructure

The essential structural framework of a country or an organization. *Public infrastructure* includes roads, bridges, drains and almost all the building construction that enables society to function. *Infrastructure* is often used as a conveniently vague word: when a politician says we must spend more on the infrastructure, it sounds as if he hasn't worked out exactly where the real priorities are.

If language is not correct, then what is said is not what is meant; if what is said is not what is meant, then what ought to be done remains undone.

Confucius

ingenious or ingenuous

Ingenious is always a *positive* word, meaning that someone or something is clever, resourceful and original. Except when used about children, *ingenuous* is usually a *negative* word, implying that someone or something is over-simple or lacking in worldliness.

inquiry or enquiry

See **enquiry**

insurance or assurance

See **assurance**

insure or ensure or assure

See **assure**

integral

Stress the *first* syllable rather than the second: 'INtegral'.

interesting

It should, of course, mean what it says – the very opposite of boring. But it has become an evasive comment on something we do not understand, or are not sure of, or don't like. If we are looking at a painting, and we don't want to make a fool of ourselves, or offend our friend who has just bought it, we fall back on 'It's very *interesting*.' The trouble is no one is taken in by it any more.

-is words

The *plural* of a number of words ending in *-is* is formed by changing the *-is* to *-es* (pron: 'eez'). These are the more common ones: analysis (pl: analyses), antithesis (pl: antitheses), basis (pl: bases), crisis, hypothesis, metamorphosis, oasis, parenthesis, synopsis, thesis. The reason is partly because of the Latin/Greek origin of the words and partly because of pronunciation – try saying 'synopsises' and you'll see why.

-ise or **-ize**

People hesitate over words like: realize, rationalize, organization, utilize, etc. The classic rule, which is followed in this book, is that if it comes from the Greek *-izein* (as it does in the words mentioned) use *-ize*. If you prefer it, you can follow the simple rule given in the official guide on English for the Civil Service, *Plain Words*: 'The simplest course is to use an "s" in all cases, for that will never be wrong, whereas "z" sometimes will be.' Current dictionaries follow the same rule: whenever they show *-ize* as an ending, *-ise* is invariably shown as an alternative. But note that where *only -ise* is indicated (compromise, disguise, enterprise, advertise, etc.), *-ize* is not an alternative.

isn't, it's, I've

See **contracted forms**. But when its is used to show possession (like *hers* or *his*), it never takes an apostrophe: '*It's* a good book' but 'Who is *its* author?'

J

jargon

Here's how Philip Howard (former literary editor of *The Times*), speaking on BBC *Woman's Hour*, put the case for and against jargon: 'Good jargon is when a specialized group of people use a kind of shorthand among themselves .... Bad *jargon* is when people do not have very much to say but dress it up to sound grand.' Remember *good jargon* in one place becomes *bad jargon* in another: *jargon* as 'expert-to-expert' language saves a lot of time, but when an expert is speaking to or writing for someone who does not hold the key to his language, he must find other ways of expressing his meaning. See **gobbledygook**

One begins to believe that a man who can write this stuff would rather eat his own typewriter than call a feeling a feeling. It must be an 'emotional experience'.

Ivor Brown, *A Word in Your Ear*

jewellery

The pronunciation of *jewellery* sorts out the *knows* from the *know-nots*. In Bond Street, home of such lordly diamond merchants as *Cartier* and *Asprey*, you will hear 'jew-el-ry'. In the Elephant and Castle, you might hear 'joo-ler-y'. Most downgrading of all is 'joolry'. *Jewelry* is an accepted alternative spelling.

jobless

A media word. I've never heard anyone actually say 'I'm jobless.'

jogging

The keep-fit craze that has spread throughout the world. They jog in Central Park, Hyde Park, on Hampstead Heath, round the Villa Borghese in Rome and in the Parc Monceau in Paris, where the French have the same word for it – *le jogging*. See **aerobic**

John Thomas

This old-fashioned expression for a penis dates from the mid-19th century. It was one of the expressions that shocked people in D.H. Lawrence's *Lady Chatterley's*

Lover, but these days it would sound almost twee. See **euphemisms**

Jones or **Joneses**

You will never keep up with them if you say you had the *Jones* for dinner. The in way of saying or writing the *plural* of Jones, Charles, Rogers and other names ending in *-s* is: Joneses, Charleses, etc.

judgement or **judgment**

Either will do but *judgement* is taking over as the more usual spelling. See **acknowledgement**

just

There is an increasing tendency, especially by TV and radio interviewers, to put *just* at the beginning of a question to make it more pointed. The difference between 'What do you mean by that?' and '*Just* what do you mean by that?' is that the second question is more aggressive or at least demanding a more detailed or less evasive answer.

K

kamikaze
The name for the Japanese 'suicide pilots' who deliberately crashed their aircraft on to enemy ships. You hear it used for any kind of reckless irresponsible decision. 'To spend so much on the scheme would be *kamikaze*.' Pron: 'kamiKAHzy'.

Keynes, Keynsian
John Maynard Keynes, the great British economist, with his advocacy of public works to reduce unemployment, is often referred to as an argument against monetarist theories. It's a gaffe to say 'Keenz'**, instead of 'Kaynz', which is correct. But note that *Milton Keynes*, the new town in north Buckinghamshire, is pronounced 'Keenz', and it's stupid affectation to say Milton 'Kaynz'.

kilometre
'SpeeDOMeter', 'baROMeter', so why not 'kiLOMeter', also with stress on second syllable? Because all metric measurements have the stress, as in French, on the first syllable: 'MILlimetre', 'CENTimetre', 'KILogram', 'KILometre' follows the same pattern. It should be added that the 'wrong'

112

pronunciation, 'kiLOMeter', has become so common that some of the latest dictionaries show it as an alternative. No stop needed after the abbreviation (kilo, kilos), and note US spelling: kilometer, etc.

kitsch

A word borrowed from German, used in art galleries about sentimental or pretentious paintings, etc. that have no real quality or genuine feeling. More recently, it is also used about novels or poetry and even films that pretend to be profound but are really aiming at popular success. Debatable taste in design can now be accused of being *kitsch*; there are people who find it fashionable to buy something for that very reason.

kneeled or **knelt**

'I *kneeled* – or I *knelt* – down'? Both are correct. *Knelt* is the more usual form in UK, *kneeled* in US.

knickers

Your grandmother might have worn *bloomers*, your mother could have worn *knickers*, but in the 21st century women, like men, wear *pants*. See **pants**

know-how

In the US, they have used *know-how* for over a hundred years. Since the late 1940s, the expression has been used in the UK and only a few isolationists still object to it as an Americanism. But it's so expressive that how could we manage without it?

kosher

The Yiddish word for food conforming to Jewish dietary laws. In New York, *not kosher* is used, by non-Jews as well as Jews, for something that is not legitimate or straightforward. TV and the theatre have brought *not kosher* to the UK, and if you are faced with an arrangement that is not above board, you can say, in the right company, 'It's *not kosher*.' See **Yinglish**

What other language is fraught with such exuberant fraughtage?

Leo Rosten, *The Joys of Yiddish*

kudos

Some people think of this word, meaning prestige or acclaim, as being plural: 'The *kudos* that are his due.' That is wrong – kudos is always *singular* ('The *kudos* that *is* his due') and there is *no* plural form. Pron: 'KOOdos' or 'KYOOdos', whichever comes naturally.

L

lad

Do we say to a young man who is annoying us: 'Now look here, my *lad*!'? Do we still describe a high-spirited man as 'Quite a lad'? If we do, then we sound middle-aged. *Lad* is not used much by younger people any more, except possibly as a defiant expression of male togetherness: 'Having a few jars with the *lads*.'

lady

The word *lady* has uncertain status. The Queen still has *ladies-in-waiting*, and MPs address a female member of parliament as *the honourable lady*. 'Charladies' have become *cleaning ladies*, some offices have *tea-ladies*; but there are 'women doctors' and 'women barristers'. In a restaurant, when a waiter asks 'Who's the duck for?', a man might answer rather lamely 'It's for the lady', because he doesn't know what else to say. It still feels right to call a woman who is very old, *an old lady*. Apart from those particular situations and a few others, most of us are more comfortable now talking about 'the woman next door', 'an interesting woman', just as D.H. Lawrence called his novel *Women in Love*. Yet because of a former distinction between *lady* and 'woman', there are some women who don't like being called *women*. Other women may object to being called *girls* (see **girl**). Meantime, we may not feel at ease calling any of them *ladies*, because the word now sounds genteel (except in particular senses where both women and men might say, for example, 'She's a very clever lady'). It's much easier in America where there's a relaxed tendency to use *ladies* for all women. But in the UK, this old 13th-century word has got itself into rather a mess. Apart from keeping to the few rules of the game, you have to sort out for yourself when to use *lady* and when not to, and hope not to offend anybody. See **girl** and **woman**

laid-back

See **cool**

last or **latter**

Latter is the second of *two* things. *Last* is the final one of *more than two*: 'There were representatives from France, Italy and Spain – the *last* was an eminent writer.'

late or ex-

At the time of writing this, Bill Clinton is the ex-President. When he dies, he will be the *late* President. See **ex**

lavatory or **toilet** or **loo**

Earlier this century, 'WC' (or 'water-closet') and 'urinal' were words in common use. They would seem quaint now, and there's a good chance that you would not even be understood. Then *lavatory* took over but is now used mostly in writing or by older people. *Toilet*, at one time considered a 'middle-class' euphemism, has become the standard formal word (with *toilet* roll and *toilet* paper), alongside the informal *loo* (and *loo* paper, etc.). *Loo* (probably from the French 'l'eau') began as an 'upper-class' expression and spread like wildfire. 'Powder-room' is coy and 'little boys' room' cringing. In the US, the usual word now, in public places, is *restroom* (a misnomer, as the writer Bel Mooney complained, when someone in Chicago banged on the door shouting 'You finished, lady?').

The upper-class accent may alter, but they are united in their absence of euphemism or circumlocution …. They would never talk about 'botties' or the 'little girls' room', or ask, as Howard Weybridge might, if they can go and 'point Percy at the Porcelain'.

Jilly Cooper, *Class*

lawyer

A useful all-embracing word that covers *barristers*, *solicitors*, and also *attorneys*, who in America combine the functions of English barristers and solicitors.

lay or **lie**

It is easy to get into a panic over which of the variants to use. The following sentences are correct: 'If you are tired, *lie* down' … 'Yesterday she was tired and *lay* down' … 'He has *lain* in bed all day' … 'The ship *lay* at anchor for a week.' When you lay an *object* down, the words are different: 'It is fragile so please *lay* it down carefully' … 'Because it was fragile, he *laid* it down carefully.' The most common mistake: 'Go and lay down', 'Tell her to lay down' (use *lie* in both cases ... see first example above).

leading question

Outside courts of law, this phrase is often used in the wrong way to mean a question that is awkward or embarrassing ('Ah – that's a *leading question* and you can't expect me to answer it'). What it does mean is a question that prompts you (or *leads* you on) to give the answer that is wanted: 'When you came home, he was already there, wasn't he?' For this reason, a judge will usually pick up a barrister for asking a witness a *leading question*.

leaped or **leapt**

Either in the UK, although *leapt* is possibly more common. *Leaped* in America. Pron: 'leaped' and 'lept'.

learned or **learnt**

Either in the UK. *Learned* is the usual form in US. See **-ed**

least or **fewest**

Least is often used wrongly: 'He had the *least* votes of all the candidates' (*fewest* is the right word there). For an easy rule, see **fewer** or **less**

lecher

It is no longer always *men* who set the pace sexually, and

while there are still *lechers* around, the word itself, like 'womanizer', doesn't seem to belong any more. But the slang abbreviation *lech*, particularly about older men ('He's an old *lech*' or 'He *leches* after young girls'), is still heard.

legal language

The drafting of legal documents has little to do with good English. We should remember that the most important consideration is that no one should ever be able to persuade a judge that the words could possibly have any other meaning than what was intended. Nevertheless, lawyers do sometimes get carried away by it all and we are faced with language that is needlessly archaic and obscure. *Clarity* is an organization, formed by solicitors, to promote clearer, more readily under-standable drafting of legal documents. Let's wish it well – after all, we should all be able to understand what we are signing.

legend or myth

A legend may stem from some historical truth (the legend of Napoleon's invincibility). A myth is entirely imaginary (it's a myth that Napoleon could foretell the future from the stars).

lend or loan

'Will you *loan* me a pen?' is not generally liked, because the word *lend* is preferred. *Loan* was used this way in the 16th century and that is still normal usage in America. Some writers in the UK feel that *loan* is appropriate where large sums of money are involved: 'The Government is *loaning* money to finance further explo-ration for North Sea oil.' Otherwise, use *lend*.

length

Remember the word 'long' and sound the 'g' lightly in *length*, rather than saying 'lenth'.

less or fewer

See **fewer**

liaise and liaison†

Not long ago, the most common meaning of *liaison*, apart from technical meanings to do with phonetics and military matters, was for a secret sexual relationship between a woman and a man. Although the 1982 *COD* gave this as the first meaning of *liaison*, we should be much more likely to say now that the couple were 'having an affair'. This leaves *liaison* available to describe any close bond or connection between organizations, ministers of governments or others in close touch over a particular problem.

libel and **slander**

Lawyers know the difference but some other people do not. *Libel* is something *written* that is untrue and damages a person's reputation; the evidence is the written or printed document. *Slander* does the same thing but it is *spoken*, so you need a witness to prove it.

libido†

You do not have to be a psychoanalyst these days to use psychological terms, and *libido* is a useful word to describe that vital inner energy that drives us on. It is thought to derive from primitive sexual energy and some schools of psychology use *libido* about only the sexual drive in humans. Jungians use *libido* in the more interesting way, as in the first sentence of this entry. Pron: 'liBEEdoh'. See **life-force**

library

Even when you're in a hurry, give it *three* syllables ('LIBRery').

licence or **license**

You may have a driving *licence* or a *licence* to sell wine. These mean that you are *licensed* to drive and *licensed* to sell wine in your *licensed* restaurant. In America, *license* covers *all* usages.

lie or **lay**

See **lay**

lieutenant

In the army, you're a 'lefTENant', in the navy, a 'leTENant'. In the US, whatever you are in, you're a 'looTENant'. The spelling stays the same.

life-force†

A simple expression, for some reason not included in all dictionaries, that explains the mysterious dynamism that makes us climb mountains, write books or at least get out of bed in the morning. Sometimes spelt with capitals: *Life-Force*. See **libido**

Somehow I have never been able to feel warmly disposed towards the Life-Force. I struggle to persuade myself that everything (and everybody) must be embraced; that the world consists of a male sky bending over a female earth; that existence should be conducted in a general uproar and that I ought to make a bonfire of my library.

> Dilys Powell, *Sunday Times* (from review
> of the film, *Zorba the Greek*)

lighted or lit

Either. Most people prefer *lit* as in: 'The fire was lit', 'the torch was lit' and use *lighted* to describe something: 'the *lighted* fire', 'the *lighted* torch'.

lightening or lightning

It is *lightning* that goes with thunder. *Lightening* is to make lighter ('lightening of burdens').

like

Some people have a vague idea it is ungrammatical to use *like* instead of 'in the same way as': 'Some girls change their lovers like they change their winter clothes.' That sentence was written by Graham Greene, and there are other good writers who are relaxed about using *like* – like that. Others would insist on 'in the same way as'. More people object to using *like* instead of 'such as', although it is very common: 'She enjoys games *like* tennis and squash.' If you want to be 'correct', change it to 'such as tennis and squash'. To use *like* in place of 'as if' *sounds* ungrammatical, and it is, so avoid 'She plays tennis *like* she enjoys it'**. Change it to '… as if she enjoys it'. But no one should ever complain when you use *like* to mean 'similar to' or 'characteristic of', as Irving Berlin did – 'There's no business like show business.'

limited

Something that is *limited* is restricted; that is, a limit is imposed: 'His overdraft is *limited* to £500.' A *Limited Company* is one in which directors have *limited* liability. The increasingly common *plc* stands for Public Limited Company. *Limited* is so often used now also to mean 'small' ('He has only a *limited* income', 'It is of only *limited* use'), that it seems pedantic to object to this. But go easy with 'a *limited* number of', which is usually no more than a pompous way of saying 'a few'.

lit or **lighted**
See **lighted**
living in sin
When Victorians said a couple were *living in sin*, it was a severe moral condemnation. Nowadays parents might say *living in sin* in order to appear light-hearted about their children's relationships. If the children, themselves, used *living in sin* about someone they are living with, it would just be a joke.
loan or **lend**
See **lend**
lobbying†
Lobbying is speaking to someone important 'in the lobby' of the House of Commons or in one of the 'corridors of power' in business or elsewhere, and persuading them to support some project or cause. A number of MPs have set themselves up as 'Government Affairs Consultants', which sounds like a euphemism for *lobbyists*, which some people consider is just another word for 'fixers'.
lonely hearts
Lonely hearts are women or men, living on their own and

wanting to meet someone as a companion or to marry. They place advertisements in the *lonely hearts* columns of newspapers and magazines, asking to meet other men and women. They go to introduction agencies, sometimes called *lonely hearts clubs*, computerized now and catering for a huge market.

lonesome
See **all alone**

loo or **lavatory** or **toilet**
See **lavatory**

lot
It is all right to use *a lot of* in serious writing: 'There were *a lot of* people there.' But *lots of* ('*Lots of* people turned up') is conversational and would be out of place in a formal context.

love
One of the most mixed-up words in English. We *love* strawberries, *love* our children, fall in *love*, make *love*, say 'thank you, *love* (or *luv*)', become over confident at tennis when the score is 40-love … and each time mean something altogether different by the word *love*. Yet even in the 21st century, *love* remains a magical disturbing word, evoking a state of happiness, distrusted and yearned for at the same time, alongside which most other things seem but a shadow.

love-hate†
A Freudian concept that seems the only way to describe an emotional response experienced by most people at times, where attraction and repulsion seem to alternate: 'A *love-hate* relationship.'

lover
In the past, if married people had other sexual relationships, the women had *lovers* and the men, 'mistresses'. *Lover* is now used freely by both men and women, whether they are married or not, about someone they are having an affair with.

For last year's words belong to last year's language
And next year's words await another voice.
                                    T.S. Eliot, *Little Gidding*

lunch or **dinner** or **supper**

A curious example of *class* distinction in English. The 'working-class' often use dinner for their midday meal, even if it's only sandwiches. For the 'middle-class', the midday meal is always *lunch* and the evening meal *dinner*. *Supper* for the 'working-class' could well be a meal at 6 pm whereas for the 'middle-class' *supper* is more likely to be after 9 pm ('Let's have *supper* after the theatre'). In Scotland, *high tea* is often the equivalent of 'working-class' *supper* in England, a meal about 6 pm. It is pretentious to use *luncheon* except for formal or official lunches. Where *luncheon vouchers* fit into that is anybody's guess.

M

MA

Stops are no longer necessary. John Brown MA – see **abbreviations**

machination

A word often in the news, because it means a plot or intrigue to do something nasty – and there's a lot of that going on in the world. The -ch- has a *k* sound (*not* like the *ch* in 'machine'): 'makiNAYshun'.

machismo and **macho**

The fashionable words to describe heavy-going masculinity, all brawn and no brain. The Spanish word *macho* is a shorter version of *machismo* and also means a man showing off his machismo. Neither word is generally complimentary. Pron: 'merTCHIZmo' and 'MATCHoh', which are nearer to the Spanish sound than 'merKISmo' and 'MAKkoh', also sometimes heard in English.

Men who try too hard to be macho are generally not mucho.
Zsa Zsa Gabor

mackintosh

For years it seemed that the Scottish inventor, Charles Macintosh, had achieved immortality, because whenever it rained, people put on a *mackintosh* (or a 'mac'). But at long last, the word is dying out and most people say 'raincoat'.

maestro

Used mostly about great composers or conductors but also extended to cover anyone who does almost anything in a masterly way. It's an Italian word (meaning master). The proper plural is *maestri* but it is so much at home in English that most people say *maestros*. Pron: 'MYSstro(s)'.

mail or **post**

You *mail* a letter in America and *post* it in the UK. When you receive letters in America, it's the mail. In the UK, we used to receive the *post* but it's not uncommon to hear 'Has the *mail* come yet?'

main street or **high street**

See **high street**

-man

A number of compound words formed with *-man-* (such as *chairman*, *mankind*, *spokesman*) have been looked at, both

in the light of the 1975 Sex Discrimination Act in Britain and out of respect for women's just expectations. Unisex words have appeared ('chairperson', 'humankind', 'spokesperson' and others) as well as alternative -*woman*-compounds (Shirley Conran called her highly successful book *Superwoman*). There is a good case for examining words that reflect sexist prejudice and it is too soon to assess where this process will lead. Inevitably it has produced some linguistic nitpicking and what one woman writer, Bel Mooney, calls 'linguistic monstrosities like herstory'. At the same time, sensible progress is being made in reducing the undeniable masculine bias in English. See **chairman**; **everybody**; **girl**; **humankind**; **sexist language**

mandatory

Not always understood. When something is *mandatory*, it is obligatory, because of a law or command from a higher authority: 'It is now *mandatory* to advertise vacancies to persons of either sex.' Stress the *first* syllable: 'MANditery' (avoid 'manDAYtery').

manipulate

To *manipulate* something is to handle it skilfully. The extended meaning, often used now, is more sinister: when someone *manipulates* a situation or, even worse, *manipulates* people, it implies exerting a cunning influence for personal advantage.

mankind

See **humankind**

manoeuvrable and **manoeuvre**

The old custom of joining the 'o' and the 'e' together into a ligature (œ) is no longer necessary, which is a relief for anyone using a wordprocessor. But remember to spell these words *oeu*, except in America where the spelling is *maneuverable* and *maneuver*.

mantra

A Sanskrit word for a Hindu or Buddhist sacred chant. *Mantras* have become familiar to more people, as the sounds or incantations used in some methods of meditation.

margarine

Manufacturers long ago gave up trying to encourage us to pronounce the 'g' as in 'Margaret'. Fears of cholesterol have helped to make *margarine* respectable and few people still degrade it by saying *marge*. Anyway people now call *margarine* by the various brand names.

marijuana

See **cannabis**

marketeer

A name for someone supporting Britain's membership of the European Community. It sounds pejorative (probably from association with black *marketeer*) but it isn't – unless you are strongly opposed to the EC.

marketing language†

Twenty-five years ago, *marketing* in the *Shorter Oxford Dictionary* was something bought and sold in the market. Since then *marketing* has become the indispensable sophisticated word for selling and takes in packaging, promotion, advertising, research, distribution and everything else in the long distance between dreaming up a new product and a 'consumer' taking it off the shelf in a supermarket. It would seem almost crude now to talk about mere 'selling'.

Marketing has developed its own go-getting language, first used by shirt-sleeved executives in the conference rooms of Madison Avenue advertising agencies. Now it is all just as familiar in the UK, where admen take a 'creative' idea and 'run it up the flagpole to see who salutes it', slot 'consumers' like you and me into 'socio-economic groups', 'package' products to 'position' them in the market and to give them 'shelf-appeal', hype them in TV commercials hoping that they will end up as 'brand leaders' rather than 'me-too' products. Marketing experts have their own arcane language to express (using Oscar Wilde's quip) the price of everything – and the value of nothing.

marketplace†

Used less now for the open space in a town where markets are held than for the general world of buying and selling: 'Let's try it out in the *marketplace*.' Hyphen is optional: *market-place* or *marketplace*. See **marketing language**

mark-up

It has *two* meanings. One is the increase in price because of inflation or extra production costs. The more usual meaning is the amount added to the cost of something to cover overheads and profit. Sometimes spelt as one word: *markup*, but clearer with a hyphen: *mark-up*.

masochism or **sadism**

Masochism is when someone gets pleasure from being hurt or humiliated. *Sadism* is to get pleasure from hurting or humiliating someone else. Although used more generally, both words relate to forms of sexual perversion, which is the usual medical connotation.

massage

On the BBC, a Labour MP spoke about the Tories '*massaging* unemployment figures'. This expressive use of *massage* suggests that figures, if not actually falsified, are 'pushed around' to make them look better. Even in the medical sense, the meaning of *massage* is sometimes stretched: 'An attractive blonde with a great sense of fun offers interesting massage in her well-equipped apartment ...' (from a recent advertisement). That may be straightforward physiotherapy, but it doesn't sound like it. In UK, stress *first* syllable: 'MASSage'; in US, stress *second*: 'massAGE'.

masterful or **masterly**

Masterful is occasionally used wrongly, particularly by sports writers who use it about an outstanding player. In that sense, the word should be *masterly*, to mean skilful and accomplished (in the manner of a master). *Masterful* means bossy and domineering: 'She is so *masterful* with him, always telling him what to do.'

may or **can**

See **can**

may or **might**

In most cases, it's easy to keep *may* and *might* in the right place. *May* refers to the present or future – *might* refers to the past: 'It may never happen', 'It might never have happened.' *Might* is also used conversationally to suggest, politely or aggressively, that someone does something: 'While you're out, you *might* do some shopping', and the classic 'You *might* help with the washing-up!'

may be or **maybe**

One word when it is an alternative to 'perhaps'; otherwise two words: '*Maybe* it is true', 'It may be true.'

me or **I**

See **I**

medecine or **medicine**

When in doubt, remember *medical*, and you'll spell it *medicine*, which is right. It's considered 'correct', at least by the BBC, to say it in two syllables: 'medsin'. But since even doctors sometimes say 'med-i-sin', we needn't fuss too much about it.

media

A convenient umbrella word covering all means of communication, such as newspapers, television and radio. It is *plural*: 'The media *are* ...' (never 'The media *is* ...'). The singular is *medium*: 'Which advertising medium was used?' The answer to that could be 'All the *media*.'

meditate and **meditation**

If someone asks you 'Do you *meditate*?', they probably no longer mean do you think long and hard about things. Another meaning of *meditation* is superseding the general meaning. *Meditation* now often refers to a spiritual exercise, a turning of attention away from oneself. The discipline spread to the West through *Transcendental Meditation* (or *TM*), which is one particular technique, developed by the maharishi who was for a time the Beatles' guru.

memoranda or memorandums

The Latin and the English plurals of *memorandum*. Both are used; *memorandums* may eventually become the standard word, alongside *memos*, more generally used and rightly now considered standard English. (Avoid 'memorandas', which is wrong and illogical, because *memoranda* is already plural.)

merchandise†

This old 13th-century word for goods that are bought and sold has another meaning in modern marketing. When a product is *merchandised*, sales are promoted through advertising, special displays and so on. *Merchandising* can be used to cover the whole spectrum of marketing from consumer research to planning advertising campaigns. Always *-ise*, never *-ize*. See **marketing language**

Messrs

The plural of 'Mr', and at one time always used before the name of a firm, as a form of address: '*Messrs* John Brown Limited'. Sedate firms of solicitors and other conservative businessmen may still use it that way. But to most people it sounds Dickensian and they've dropped it.

metaphysics and metaphysical†

Words that are often used with only a vague idea of what they mean. *Metaphysics* is the title of a treatise by the Greek philosopher, Aristotle (384-322 BC), in which he dealt with the nature of being. The 17th-century Metaphysical Poets, notably John Donne, were concerned with this philosophy. *Metaphysical* came to be misused to describe ideas and revelations that transcend the external physical world, and almost as a synonym for 'mystical'. Apart from academic philosophy, this is how *metaphysics* and *metaphysical* are usually used now, for concepts that are intangible, which relate to another kind of reality, more real, some believe, than the seeming reality of the world around us.

methodology

Criticized by some writers as an unnecessary modish '-ology' word that means no more than 'method'. For others *methodology* is a useful word, implying a more detailed

analysis of principles and suggesting a more scientific approach than 'method': 'The *methodology* of marketing'.
meticulous
Be careful about using this word, as it is often used now to mean careful and detailed, in a good way. Its proper meaning is fussy and pernickety, an over-attention to detail: 'Such a *meticulous* examination of the proposals wastes everyone's time.'

Many writers perplexe their Readers, and Hearers with meere Non-sense. *Their writings need sunshine ... A barbarous Phrase hath often made mee out of love with a good sense; and doubtfull writing hath wrackt mee beyond my patience.*
Ben Jonson (1572-1637), *Timber*

metric
The UK is now metric but many people are still not at home with all the new units of measurement. 'A miss is as good as *1.609* kilometres' does not sound quite the same. Willard R. Espy quotes Walter Sullivan in the *New York Times*: 'Will angry men cry: *I'll beat you to within a centimeter of your life*? Or *Give him a millimeter and he'll take a kilometer*?' See **kilometre**
mileage†
Mileage is the number of miles travelled. This meaning has become extended to cover the extent of usefulness or profitability of a product or an event: 'We want to get as much mileage as possible out of the advertising.'
militate or **mitigate**
Mitigate is often used wrongly instead of *militate*. The two words have different meanings. When something is *mitigated*, the bad effects are lessened: 'The effects of the famine will be *mitigated* by worldwide aid.' *Militate* is connected with the word 'military' and means to 'go against something': 'His casual appearance *militated* against people taking him seriously.' It's a good rule never to write or say: *mitigate against*.
millennium
A *millennium* = 1000 years. Two *millennia* or two *milleniums* = 2000 years, and so on. It's easy to slip up and spell it with one -*n*-, so remember millennium.

mini-

Although *mini-* was already in use for something that is a 'miniature' of something else, it was the *mini-skirt*, Mary Quant's symbol of the 1960s, that made *mini-* take off as a useful prefix. It's still available for anyone to attach to anything that is a smaller version of the real thing. Chemists sell *mini-meals* for slimmers, the chancellor presents *mini-budgets* between his main budgets, just as Sir Alec Issigonis made a breakthrough in car design with the *Mini* (with a capital 'M').

miniscule or **minuscule**

Because of the strong pull of the prefix 'mini-', *minuscule* is often misspelt as 'miniscule'. Pron: 'MINNaskyool'.

missile

Wherever you are, you cannot get away from this word and its sinister implications. Americans usually pronounce it 'MISSle' (rhyming with 'whistle'); we say 'MISSeyle' (last syllable rhyming with 'mile'), which is the standard UK pronunciation.

mistress

A word on its way into oblivion. A man would now usually call his mistress his 'lover'. Even *headmistresses* are becoming 'headteachers'. See **boyfriend** and **lover**

> *Oh mistress mine! Where are you roaming?*
> *Oh stay and hear – your true love's coming …*
> Shakespeare, *Twelfth Night*

moment of truth†

The *moment of truth* is any situation when the chips are down and bluffing will get you nowhere. It is a good phrase, translated from the Spanish *el momento de la verdad*, the moment in a bullfight, described by Ernest Hemingway (in *Death in the Afternoon*) as '… the final sword thrust, the actual encounter between the man and the animal …'.

monetarism

The economic theory which is based on the belief that if you control the supply of money, you can control the economy, and is the opposite to 'spending your way' out of unemployment and recession. In the UK, it has been successful in reducing inflation and increasing unemployment, which is why it is so controversial. An idea or a theory is monetarist (not monetaristic).

moonlighting

A rather poetic word to describe the practice of doing a second job, usually in the evening, in addition to holding down a normal full-time job.

more or **most**

Use *more* about *two* people or things: 'It is difficult to say which of the two of them is more confused.' Use *most* about more than two: 'It's difficult to say which MPs in the House were the *most* angry.'

mortgage

A big *mortgage* is bad enough without pronouncing it wrongly. The *-t-* is not sounded: 'MORgidge'.

movie

When characters on film seemed to *move*, Americans called them 'moving pictures' and then *movies*. The word crossed the Atlantic as long ago as 1913, according to Eric Partridge. Now people talk about going to see a *film*. Some older people may say 'Let's go to the *pictures*.'

Flicks has died a death. On TV and video-recorders, *movies* have become video-films or simply *videos*. The American *movie-theatre* has been successfully resisted in the UK and *cinema* remains the usual British word (classically correct since it comes from Greek *kinema*, meaning 'movement'). But the official film institution in the UK looks across to Hollywood and calls itself 'The National Film Theatre'.

Mr and Mrs

It is unnecessary now to put stops after Mr and Mrs – see **abbreviations**

Language, be it remembered, is not an abstract construction of the learned, or of dictionary-makers, but is something arising out of the work, needs, ties, joys, affections, tastes, of long generations of humanity, and has its bases broad and low, close to the ground.

Walt Whitman, *The North American Review* (1885)

Ms

The idea originally was to have a title that was neither Mrs nor Miss. Ms had a hostile reception, from women as well as men, when it first appeared. B.A. Phythian, in his *Dictionary of Correct English* (1979), proclaimed: 'The word is foolish, ugly, meaningless and almost unpronounceable, and deserves oblivion.' Yet it is fair and reasonable that women, like men, should have available a form of address not linked to their marital status. Ms has gained some acceptance: it is used by 'serious' newspapers, such as the *Observer*, and is officially accepted in the House of Commons for women MPs, if they wish to use it. It has also proved useful for writing to women and the old question 'Is it Mrs or Miss?' sometimes gets a firm rebuff. It must be added that many women do not want to be called *Ms* and that it is not easy to use unselfconsciously in speech. The accepted pronunciations are 'mizz' or 'merz', with 'merz' in the lead. *Ms* is here to stay and should be used to address women who prefer it, although it is uncertain how much more progress it will make towards becoming the universal form of address for a woman. As an alternative, it is more and more usual to introduce women and men without using a title: 'Mary Brown, the well-known author, is going to talk to us', 'Let me introduce you – this is John Brown.' This egalitarian approach fits in with the relaxed style of the times.

multinational

While it still means something that involves a number of nations ('A *multinational* plan for famine relief'), a *multinational* is also the word for a powerful commercial conglomerate, such as *Coca-Cola*, whose organization is world-wide.

municipal

Stress the *second* syllable not the first: 'mewNISSsiple' (not 'MEWnissiple', which is often heard).

muscle†

'Muscle-men' are gangsters whose job it is to throw their weight around. Perhaps from that use, *muscle* has become extended to cover the heavy-weight power to make things happen. We hear, for example, of the *marketing muscle* of companies and the *political muscle* of influential politicians. Big businesses can *muscle* aside competition.

Muslim

A *Muslim* is a follower of the faith of Islam. Use this word (always with a capital 'M') instead of 'Moslem', which is not liked. Pron: usually 'MOOZlim' but 'MUZZlim' is also heard. When speaking about culture, 'Islamic' should be used, as in 'Islamic art'.

mutual

After Charles Dickens called his famous novel *Our Mutual Friend*, it is difficult to argue, as some still do, that mutual should not be used about something we have in common with someone else, but only about reciprocal feelings: 'The *mutual* love of father and daughter', that is, their love for each other. Yet even purists admit that *mutual* should be used instead of 'common' to avoid a possible misunderstanding. As Dickens probably realized, 'our common friend' could mean our low-class friend. In situations like that, *mutual* gets us off the hook. See **common**

myself

> *Myself* is often used, rather pretentiously, when all that is needed is a simple *I* or *me*: 'Please contact *myself* over this', 'Another director and *myself* will be coming to the meeting.' Why not 'Please contact *me* …', 'Another director and *I* …'? See **I** or **me**

mystique

> In English, *mystique* has become a fashionable word for a popular myth or illusion built up about somebody or something by clever publicity or through great popular appeal. Ordinary people, who find themselves presidents of countries, desperately need this kind of *mystique*, and some experts enhance their reputations (and their fees) by implying a *mystique* about their abilities. *Mystique* is now a doubled-edged word that can mean something mystical or supernatural but often suggests something phoney and manufactured. See **charisma**

N

nadir and **zenith**

Properly used about points in the heavens: the *zenith* of the sun is the point at which the sun is at its highest, directly above the observer; *nadir* is the opposite, when a point in the heavens is at its lowest. Both words are used about the fortunes of men and women, of governments, of the economy or about almost anything where the wheel of fortune turns: *zenith* when something is at its peak, *nadir* (pron: 'nahdeer' or 'naydeer') when it hits rock bottom.

NASA

There is a whole new language of *acronyms*, which is the name for words formed out of the initial letters of titles, usually of organizations. This is common on the international scene as in UNO ('yoonoh'), UNESCO ('yoonesco'). NASA ('nasser') is often heard on news programmes, in connection with rocket and satellite launches, yet some people, especially in the UK, are not sure what it means. It is the US *National Aeronautics and Space Administration*.

native

Although, of course, anyone is a *native* of the place where they are born, whether it is London or Texas, the word has old colonial associations with tribal war-dances, cannibals and what were regarded as 'inferior' races ('The natives were friendly'). *Native* could understandably give offence now if it is used without thought. See **negro, racist words**

The word is half his that speaks it and half his that hears it.
Montaigne, *Essays*

natural and **real**

Artificial substitutes have become the norm for so many things, that we now have to use *natural* or *real* to emphasize that we want 'the real thing': a *natural* sponge, *natural* wood, *real* coffee, *real* cotton. A *natural* is someone who does something, from playing football to acting, as effortlessly as breathing; this expressive usage is considered colloquial by some authorities, though rightly treated as standard by the *COD*. But it is slang usage to

137

call a scheme or a product *a natural*, meaning it is bound to succeed.

naturist

The word 'nudist' is not used much now because, as a BBC reporter said, 'nude' rhymes with lewd, rude and crude. If you enjoy walking around naked, the *in* word is *naturist* (pron: 'NAYcherist'), which has a nice comfortable feeling of living naturally and simply. No one cares if it makes all the rest of us 'unnaturists'. With words, it's every man or woman for themselves.

naughty

It's all right, provided you are not sowing seeds of hangups, to use *naughty* to or about children. In other ways, *naughty* has become sickeningly arch and coy. Strip shows are called '*naughty* shows' (or even more sexploitive, '*naughty* but nice'), women's frilly panties are *naughty*; and *naughty* is used by some women and men about almost any kind of sexual approach. But the last word on naughty belongs to 1984 *LD* which quotes 'Don't forget to scrub your *naughty* bits!'

necessarily

Current dictionaries offer the choice between putting the stress on the *first* syllable ('NECessarily'), traditionally 'correct' in the UK, and the American way of putting the stress on the third syllable ('necesSARily'). 'NecesSARily' is easier to say, but to some people in the UK, 'NECessarily' still shows you know what's what.

negotiate

Authorities agree that you can use the *sh* or the *s* sound: 'neGOSHiate' *or* 'neGOHSsiate'.

negro

It is a legitimate word for a member of the black African races but in the US it has for a long time been a sensitive word, disliked by black people. This now also applies in the UK and *negro* should be avoided, as a word that will give offence. See **black** and **racist words**

neither ... nor

'Neither ... nor' is standard and 'neither ... or' is wrong. It is not true, as some books still lay down, that '*neither ... nor*' should be used about only *two* alternatives. You can say 'Neither Mary, nor John, nor Harry, nor Susan turned up.' There are other difficulties connected with *neither ... nor* and these are dealt with under **either**. Pron: 'neyether' or 'neether'. But in America, always 'neether'.

neo-

Neo- can be attached (always with a hyphen) to philo-sophies, schools of thought, ideas and to almost anything else to indicate a revival or a revised or adapted version of them: neo-classical, neo-Freudian, neo-Nazi.

neurotic

There is a medical distinction between neurotic, which means suffering from a nervous *disease*, and 'neuras-thenic', which is no more than a nervous weakness. But instead of leaving *neurotic* to doctors, many people use it casually about anyone over-anxious or worried, or about the mildest of hang-ups. 'The meaning of neurotic has become so vague,' Dr Margaret Wright says, 'that psych-iatrists seldom use it any more.'

nice

It has been fashionable for years to criticize *nice* as an over-used non-committal word for anything that is pleas-ant or agreeable. It is probably true that people do use this maid-of-all-work word too often. But we shouldn't fuss too much about it: sometimes it is 'a *nice* day' because someone has been '*nice* to us' ... and everyone knows what we mean.

night or **night-**

Nearly always hyphenated when joined to another word: night-cap, night-club, night-dress, night-life, night-light, night-shift, night-work, night-watchman. But not at *nightfall* or when you have a *nightmare*.

nirvana†

A Sanskrit word that people in the West hear, with little understanding of what it means, when they are attracted to Buddhism or to one of the schools of meditation that promise enlightenment. *Nirvana* cannot be understood until it is experienced: it is, beyond all, a freedom from self, from our agonized holding on to individuality and desires.

nitty-gritty

No one knows the origin of these words. When you get down to the *nitty-gritty* with someone, there is a narrowing of the eyes, a squaring of the jaw, because polite conversation is over and you are about to deal with the hard facts, whether people like them or not. The expression is written off as *slang* by most dictionaries, which is a pity because; as well as being useful, *nitty-gritty* actually has the sound of what it means – and you can't ask more from language than that.

nobody

See **everybody**

non-

Non- is a simple way of making some words mean the opposite: *non-appearance, non-existent.* Although they are frequently written without a hyphen, *non-* words are usually clearer with one: non-alcoholic (rather than 'nonalcoholic'), *non-event* (rather than 'nonevent'), but there is no consistent rule. Be careful about the difference that can arise between *non-* and *un-*: *non-* is a simple negative, whereas *un-* can add a pejorative meaning: *non-scientific* means not connected with science, *unscientific* can mean slipshod because science has not been taken into account; *non-informed* means not having the information, *uninformed* can mean ignorant.

none is or **none are**

It all started with the belief that none equals not one and so is *singular*: 'None of the members is present.' Weighty authorities, such as Fowler, Partridge and the *Oxford English Dictionary*, refute this: the *OED* even adds that it is more usual to write 'none *are* ...'. Use *none is* or *none are*, whichever seems right to you in a particular sentence, and if anyone objects, throw all twenty volumes of the *Oxford English Dictionary* at them.

non-U

See **class language**

no one or **no-one** or **noone**

No one is the form recommended by most dictionaries. See **everybody**

north, south, east and **west**

You can go *south* or face a *north* wind, without using capitals. Whenever a *region* is designated, use a capital: 'the mysterious East', 'the weather in the West', 'trade barriers between East and West'. Abbreviations: N, W, SE, NW, etc.

nosh

This Yiddish word has crossed so many frontiers that one would expect even an archbishop to use it – in off-duty moments, of course. Originally it meant something tasty between meals, now it simply means something to eat. A *nosh-up* means a lot to eat. No modern dictionary can leave out *nosh*, the most popular slang word that Yiddish has donated to English.

English ... has zestfully borrowed a marvellous gallimaufry of foreign locutions, including many from Yiddish; and who will deny that such brigandage has vastly enriched our cherished tongue?

Leo Rosten, *The Joys of Yiddish*

not

One of the trickiest words in English. The argument is that two *nots* make a *yes* – the old bugbear of the double negative. Language is not mathematics and great writers, including Chaucer and Shakespeare, have written in an extra not, to increase the intensity of the negative. Nevertheless, 'I don't know nothing about it'*** is regarded as ill-educated, although we understand what it means. 'Hardly' and 'scarcely' are words with a built-in negative and if an extra *not* is allowed to creep in, as often happens, the result is a double negative: 'He hadn't scarcely any food left'**, 'I couldn't hardly see anything'**. The *not* should be left out: 'He had scarcely any food left', 'I could hardly see anything'. See **hardly**

no way**

Many people in the UK dislike *no way* as an abbreviation for 'there is no way ...' and 'in no way ...': 'Can you give us a discount?' – '*No way*', '*No way* is it possible.' Even in America, where *no way* is often used in these ways, it is nearer to slang than to standard usage.

nudist

See **naturist**

number of

'A *number* of books *is* on the table' or '... *are* on the table'? For once, there is an easy rule: *a number* is *plural*, followed by 'are', 'have', etc.; *the number* is *singular*, followed by 'is', 'has', etc.: '*A number* of women *are* coming tonight', '*The number* of women who will be here *is* small.'

O

oculist or **optician** and **ophthalmic**

These terms have become mixed up. At one time, an *oculist* was normally a medical specialist dealing in eye disorders, who prescribed lenses which an *optician* made up into glasses. Now *opticians* are often called *oculists* and doctors who are eye specialists usually call themselves ophthalmic surgeons or, less commonly, *ophthalmologists*. To make it more complicated, *opticians* qualified to test eyesight and prescribe lenses, as many of them are, sometimes adopt the grand title of *ophthalmic opticians*, which does not mean they are qualified doctors. *Ophthalmic* – a difficult word to spell and pronounce unless you look at it closely. Pron: 'offTHALmic' (*not* 'opTHALmic').

odd

Compare these two sentences and you'll see how a well-placed *hyphen* can avoid a possible misunderstanding: 'There were some 50 *odd* people there', 'There were some *50-odd* people there.'

Oedipus

In Greek mythology, *Oedipus* unknowingly killed his father and married his mother. In the 5th century BC,

Sophocles used the story for a great tragedy. In the 21st century, an *Oedipus complex* (pron. 'EEdipus') is when a son is sexually attracted to his mother or is too much under her influence.

Oedipus ... Schmoedipus ... What does it matter so long as he loves his mother?

Attributed to Sam Goldwyn

off

No offence is intended to those people who still say 'orff', but it does sound affected and even the most aristocratic BBC announcers are asked to avoid it.

off-beat or **off-key**

Two musical terms that work well in everyday language but should not be confused. *Off-beat* describes anyone or anything, often interesting or amusing, that is not in line with the usual order of things. Some dictionaries show it as one word (*offbeat*) but it's better with a hyphen: *off-beat*. The *LD* regards *off-beat* as 'informal' but the *COD* admits it as standard English. *Off-key* also describes something that is out of line, but in an unpleasant jarring way.

off of

Don't take anything *off of* anything – just take it *off*. Apart from sounding funny, *off of* is wrong, since the one word *off* says it all.

often

To pronounce the 't' (instead of making it rhyme with 'soften') used to be considered as vulgar as eating peas off a knife. The 't' is sounded in America and heard so often now in the UK that the time has come when 'offen' sounds old-fashioned. At present you can still choose for yourself, as current dictionaries show both pronunciations. However, 'awfen', still heard, sounds distinctly 'orf'.

... the conviction seems now to be almost universal that when one is before a microphone or on a platform the dignity of one's position demands the articulation of the 't' in 'often'.

Sir Ernest Gowers, presidential address to
the English Association

ombudsman

A word, borrowed from Swedish about 40 years ago, for someone officially appointed to investigate complaints from the public against official bodies. Pron: 'OMMboodsman'.

on

Whatever anyone says, 'What did you put it *on*?' is good English. See **prepositions at end of sentences**

on or **upon**

Some people bend over backwards to use these words in slightly different ways. It's not worth bothering about, except to keep to certain established usages, such as *on account*, since *on* and *upon* are interchangeable. Perhaps *upon* sounds more formal and dignified, but it is becoming old-fashioned.

one

The trouble is that once you start using one, you have to stay with it: '*One* shouldn't say to *one's* wife, when *one* comes home late from *one's* office, that *one* was having a drink with *one's* friends.' It is not good English to switch from *one* to 'you': '*One* shouldn't say to *your* wife ....' So think twice before committing yourself to *one*.

one another

See **each other**

one of

'*One of* the travellers has lost *his* baggage.' But what if the traveller turns out to be a woman? See **everybody**

ongoing

Ongoing still comes in for some stick. For one writer, it is 'an over-used, pretentious and totally unnecessary substitute for *continuing*, and ought to be shunned'. An Oxford writer on English usage is more generous, comparing *ongoing* with 'oncoming', and considering it useful to describe something that 'goes on'. Many people find *ongoing* more direct and immediate than 'continuing': 'The *ongoing* problem of unemployment ....' It's a matter of taste but be warned that there are still a few people who will hate you for going on using *ongoing*.

only

There are fusspots who deny that 'We *only* live once'

and insist on 'We live *only* once'. *Only*, they say, must always come immediately in front of the word it refers to. Fowler says such pedants want to 'turn English into an exact science or an automatic machine'. Language doesn't work that way, and everyone knows what we mean by 'I *only* want one glass of wine' (instead of '... *only* one glass ...'). Certainly we can be relaxed about *only*, in conversation, because our tone will make it clear what we mean. In writing, we should be more careful if there's a risk of misunderstanding. Many good writers, such as Doris Lessing, Kingsley Amis, Graham Greene, Evelyn Waugh and George Orwell, are not at all fussed about placing *only* wherever it suits them: 'The captain ... only appeared once at table' (Graham Greene), rather than '... appeared only once....'

Perhaps the most misplaced word in English is the humble and peripatetic 'only'. Idiom does, of course, produce exceptions to the rule. 'I have eyes only for you' (instead of 'I only have eyes for you') would make a lousy song.
William Connolly in the *New York Times*

on to or **onto**
Onto, as one word, appears in print and some people distinguish between 'Let's go *on to* the next pub' and 'Put it *onto* the table.' The latest Oxford view is that the one word version, *onto*, should not be used at all. That's the present state of play.

OPEC
This acronym (the name for a word formed out of initial letters of titles) keeps coming into the news, as OPEC's decisions can affect world economy. Pronounced 'OHPpeck', it stands for *Organization of Petroleum Exporting Countries*. At the time of writing, Britain is not a member.

optimal and **optimum**
Often used wrongly and misleadingly for simply the biggest or the most: 'The *optimum* return is 10% p.a.', meaning the highest return available. *Optimum* does

mean the most, but always taking into account the conflicting factors involved. We should refer to '*optimum* return' only if we mean the highest return available, *consistent with* financial security, reasonable access to capital, or whatever other factors are specified. *Optimal* means exactly the same as *optimum* and should be used in the same way.

or

No matter how many *ors* there are in a sentence, it is *singular*: 'John or Mary or Helen *is* coming to look after me.' It helps a reader to insert a comma before *or*, where *or* links the last two items of a list: 'green, blue, yellow, pink, *or* red'.

-or or **-our**

In America, *-or* is standard in nearly all words that take *-our* in the UK: humor, color, labor, odor and so on.

oral or **verbal**

This is an old confusion, written about in every book on English. Yet most people talk about a '*verbal* agreement' meaning an agreement not written down. The fact is *all* agreements using words, either in speech or in writing, are *verbal* agreements. *Verbal* means words. An agreement spoken about but not written down is strictly an *oral* agreement, just as an *oral* examination is an examination conducted by the examiner and student *talking* to each other. But this is a lost cause.

orchestra

'The orchestra *is* about to play' but 'the orchestra *are* having their lunch'. See **board**

orient or **orientate**

Both words mean the same, originally to face or turn towards the East. If we are lost, we try to *orientate* ourselves, that is, to find our bearings. These meanings have become extended and the fashionable use now, not yet accepted by all dictionaries, is to say someone or something is biased in a particular direction: ad agencies say they are *client-oriented*, a new model of a car claims to be *oriented* towards safety or safety-orientated. *Orient* and *orientate* are used so often that it is worth considering alternatives such as 'aimed at' or 'directed towards'.

Oscar†

Oscars are the statuettes presented at Hollywood extravaganzas and awarded by the American Academy of Motion Picture Arts and Sciences. Why *Oscar*? The accepted reason is that a member of the Academy once looked at a statuette and declared 'My! It's just like my Uncle Oscar.' *Oscar* is also now used for any kind of success: 'She gets an *Oscar* for her cheese soufflé!' In the UK, annual awards for achievements in the theatre are called the *Laurence Olivier Awards*, and when they were presented for the first time, Joan Plowright (Lady Olivier) said she hoped one day they would be called the *Larrys*. It hasn't happened yet, but stand by for a new word to enter the English language.

Ours or our's

Our's is *always* wrong.

outline or summary

There is a distinction here worth preserving. An *outline* is an indication of the overall form of a plan, a book, or a project, sometimes prepared before the details have been worked out, and the purpose is to convey the general idea, perhaps to get approval in principle. A *summary* is an abbreviated version of something that includes essential detail, and the purpose is to save a reader time and trouble or to recapitulate the main points.

over or **over-**

Many compound words are formed with *over*. The majority do not need a hyphen: overact, overblown, oversight, overwork, etc. Some of the common ones that are better with a hyphen are: over-active, over-careful, over-confident, over-produce, over-react, over-sexed, over-simplify, over-subscribe. But this is a matter of opinion and the tendency is to drop the hyphen. If in doubt – leave it out.

Oxbridge

The standard expression, used in educational contexts, to refer to the two ancient universities, Oxford and Cambridge. It distinguishes them from *Redbrick*, which refers to most of the modern universities.

Oxford

The incomparable *Oxford English Dictionary* (known as the *OED*) was conceived in 1858 and not finished until 1928. The 20 volumes of the latest edition give pronouncements from Oxford about the English language stature and weight. But always remember that so much to do with English is a matter of opinion. The members of the Oxford English Dictionary Department spend much of their lives absorbed in the mechanics of English, in 'the *how* instead of the *what*', as the distinguished novelist, Bernice Rubens, once said. At times, they may not be switched on to the creative power of the language, and we do not always have to accept their judgements. But everyone who uses English should be grateful to the lexicographers of Oxford, and I take this opportunity to salute them.

Dictionaries are among the noblest ventures of man the ordering animal, the only signposts we have in the great forest of words through which we wander all our lives.

Gerald Long, BBC Radio 3

P

pacemaker or **pacesetter**†

Interchangeable words for someone who sets the pace for someone else to keep up with, in a race or in training. Also for someone who takes the lead in an enterprise: 'The marketing director is the *pacesetter* in the export drive.' But only pacemaker is used for the electronic device implanted surgically to regulate the heartbeat. *Pace-maker* and *pace-setter* in some dictionaries, but the tendency now is to drop the hyphen.

pajamas or **pyjamas**

In London men sleep in *pyjamas*, in New York – *pajamas*.

panda

The small police cars, used in towns in the UK, used to be black and white, like the pandas you see in the zoo. Although the colour of the cars has changed, they're still occasionally called *panda* cars.

pansy

When you mean the flower with velvety petals, that's all right. But if you are still using *pansy* to mean a homosexual, you'd better turn to the entry in this book for **gay**.

pants

It would sound Dickensian to go into a shop and ask for 'underpants'. *Pants* is the standard word used by men and (sometimes via the diminutive *panties*) by women. *Pants* are 'an undergarment that covers the crotch and hips and that may extend to the waist and partly down each leg' (*LD*), so it's not surprising that many young people have switched to *briefs*, using *pants*, as the Americans do, for trousers. But *trousers* remains the most common word in the UK, except when someone 'bores the pants off us'. See **knickers**

paragraphs

In the early 1920s, apart from talking to people, the usual way to take in information was through printed words. But now far more people take in far more information through sound and pictures than in any other way. We have all become used to an electronic immediacy and long paragraphs can be off-putting. The tendency is for shorter and shorter paragraphs in books, newspapers and letters, almost to the point sometimes where each sentence has a paragraph to itself. The result can be rather breathless and jerky. Longer paragraphs (although not too long), like talking more slowly, can encourage people to take us more seriously. When it's time to start a new train of thought, and a *full stop* isn't a big enough break from what has gone before, that's the moment to start a *new paragraph*. But think of the reader and don't wait too long. See **punctuation**

parallel

If you sometimes hesitate over how to spell this word, think of the two 'lls' being – *parallel*. Remember also that the final 'l' is not doubled in *paralleled* or *unparalleled*.

parameter

Correctly used in abstruse mathematical or technical contexts. The fashionable and showy use of *parameters* to mean 'limits' or 'framework' ('This report deals with the problem within certain parameters') is pretentious and confuses the word with 'perimeters'. A 'perimeter' is the boundary of an area. The meaning could be stretched, and if you really must have a grander word than 'limits', 'perimeters' would at least make more sense than *parameters*.

Parkinson's Law

Any job of work will take just as long as the time available to do it. That is *Parkinson's Law*. The expression has entered English, is now found in most dictionaries, and has brought immortality to Northcote Parkinson, who first made this shrewd observation on human nature.

passed or **past**

These examples explain all you need to know: I *passed* by your window. I have *passed* your window many times. I have just gone *past* your window. In the *past* week, I *passed* your window every day.

'pee' or **pence**

When decimalization of UK currency was introduced, shopkeepers and most of their customers started to say *pee* instead of *pence*, consciously or unconsciously distinguishing the new basic unit from the former one. Although BBC announcers are asked to say *pence*, most people say *pee*, to remind us that things have changed since *The Times* or a pint of milk cost five old *pence* (about 2p). Whether it's a *penny*, *pence* or *pee*, no stop is required after p: 50p

pentagon

A *pentagon* is a five-sided shape or building. Give it a capital 'P' and the security of the world depends upon it – the *Pentagon* is the headquarters of US defence forces.

permissive

Permissive has become for some people a word of abuse, symbolizing decadence, sexual perversion and the negation of everything that is 'good'. For others it represents a long overdue breaking down of rigid authoritarian values. Depending upon how you see it, or perhaps how old you are, the *permissive society* is an 'anything goes' society or a liberated society with more opportunities to explore human experience. So *permissive* is a word to use with care.

petrol

Two compound words, using petrol, are often in the news. A *petrol bomb* is a crude hand grenade, made by filling a bottle with petrol, leaving a piece of rag dangling out of it to act as a fuse. *Petro-currency*, which has not yet found its way into all dictionaries, is the currency of a country, such as the UK, whose economy is partly dependent on the export of petrol. The price of oil is quoted in US dollars and *petro-dollars* are the dollars available in a petroleum-exporting country. See **gas**

phantasy or **fantasy**
See **fantasy**

phenomenon or **phenomena**
This *phenomenon* (singular) – these *phenomena* (plural). People often say 'a phenomena' when they mean a *phenomenon*.

philosophy
This august word for the pursuit of wisdom, that brings to mind some of the greatest thinkers who have ever lived, has been turned into an ordinary everyday word. *Philosophy* is now used for the principles or theory of almost anything: 'What is the marketing *philosophy* behind the scheme?', 'My fundamental philosophy about pruning roses is ....' A noble word has fallen into banality.

'The question is,' said Alice, 'whether you can make words mean so many different things.'
Lewis Carroll, *Through the Looking-Glass*

phone or **'phone**
'Phone is obsolete (see **flu**). Most Oxford dictionaries still regard *phone* as conversational rather than for written use, although *phone* is used in Parliament and by the BBC (*phone-tapping, phone-in*).

phoney or **phony**
Usually *phoney* in UK and *phony* in America. Not always accepted as standard English but invaluable for describing someone ('a phoney') or something ('a *phoney* name') that is not genuine.

pictures
See **movie**

pill or **tablet**
Pill has become so closely associated with oral contraceptives that it is less confusing now to call all other pills – *tablets*.

piss and **pee**
Apparently it is all right to say you are going for a *pee*, for that is normal colloquial English (*COD*). But *piss*, the dictionaries tell us, is a vulgar four-letter word. See **four-letter words**

The 'Saxon' words for 'to urinate' and 'to defecate' are idiomatic, and perfect English, but association and prudery put them into quarantine.

Eric Partridge, *Usage and Abusage*

plastic

The 'posh' pronunciation used to be 'plahstic' which could now sound affected. Standard pronunciation makes it rhyme with 'fantastic'.

plastic money

Most dictionaries have caught up with this descriptive expression for credit cards: 'Can I pay with *plastic money*?' Although generally people now say *credit card*.

Platonic

A *platonic friendship* has little to do with the Greek philosopher, Plato (428-347 BC). For most people it means a friendship between a woman and a man, without them being involved sexually. Used in that way, as an ordinary word, platonic is often spelt with a small 'p'.

plebeian

A notorious word for tripping people up over the spelling, because of the 'e' after the 'b'. If you forget, you can always write *pleb* (although it is considered slang by some dictionaries) for someone who is really common.

pleonasm

Pleonasm (pron: 'PLEEernasm') means using unnecessary words: 'I saw it with my own eyes.' 'Ha!' cry the nitpickers. 'How else could you have seen it?' But the extra words do add an intensity to the statement. Too many words *are* used too often and this can be tedious and boring. Yet language is not a mechanical '2+2=4' business, and some of the best writers use more words than are strictly necessary in order to convey feeling and nuances. But please do *not* take that as the green light to use all the words that come into your head – nearly everything that is written or said could be improved by cutting. See **tautology** and **verbosity**

pornography

This was Mary Whitehouse, in her submission to the Annan Committee on Broadcasting: 'The essence of sex is that it is a private personal experience between two people.' Presumably, for many people, almost anything outside those limits could be *pornography*. Art and literature, essentially involved with exploring the human situation, could hardly leave out sex. *Lady Chatterley's Lover* is now officially 'literature' rather than *pornography*. What about Edouard Manet's famous painting, *Déjeuner sur l'herbe*, depicting a sexy young woman lounging stark naked on the grass among elegantly dressed gentlemen? Where do art and an explicit interest in the sexual drive stop and *pornography* begin? In the 21st century the answer to that is so uncertain that whenever we use *pornography*, *pornographic* or *porn*, we may be walking on thin ice.

posh

This is considered slang, or at least informal English. Yet Sir Robin Day, on BBC *The World at One*, spoke about 'the *posher* papers'. Who could blame him, because nothing else says it quite as well? If you're stuck for an alternative, try 'grand' (or 'classy', although that's also considered informal).

post or mail

See **mail**

pot

See **cannabis**

p.p.

When a secretary signed for her boss, she used to put *p.p.* (Latin *per pro* – 'on behalf of') in front of his name. That is becoming much less common and it is more usual now to put *for* in front of the name of someone you are signing for. Why not?

practice or **practise**

This is an old linguistic chestnut, yet many of us still hesitate over which to use. '*Practise* the piano because *practice* makes perfect', 'A doctor *practises* medicine in his *practice*.' It may help to remember 'device' and 'devise' which are used in correspondingly different ways. In America, there's no problem, because both words are spelt *practice*.

prepositions at end of sentences

A *preposition* is a word, usually a short one, that links one word or phrase to another: 'She went *to* the door ... *into* the house ... *up* the stairs.' *Preposition* comes from Latin, meaning 'to go before', and from that stems the hackneyed worn-out rule that we must never end a sentence with *to*, *from*, *for*, *with*, *up*, or any other *preposition*. If you feel that way, go on saying 'At which hotel are you staying?', '*Into* which box did you put it?', '*From* where does it come?' But you will sound unnatural, as even the most cautious grammarian now accepts that it is perfectly good English to *end a sentence with a preposition*, when that is the natural place for it.

When I read some of the rules for speaking and writing the English language correctly, I think –
> *Any fool can make a rule*
> *And every fool will mind it*!

Henry David Thoreau, *Journal*,
3 February 1860

pressurize

One of the *-ize* words that some people object to because, they say, it is properly used about gases or liquids contained under pressure. Many words from one field are freely adapted to another, and Sir Bruce Fraser, in *Plain Words*, finds *pressurize* valid and useful for describing a person put under pressure: 'He *pressurized* the minister to raise the matter in the House.'

presumptious or **presumptuous**

Presumptious is often written and said, although it is wrong. *Presumptuous* should be used and pronounced 'preZUMP-chew-us' (*not* 'preZUMPshus').

primarily

In the UK, stress first syllable: 'PRIMEerily'. In America, second syllable: 'primeARRrily'.

Prime Minister or **prime minister**

Usually capitals to refer to the holder of the office and small letters for former ones. Margaret Thatcher was *Prime Minister*, but now she is a former *prime minister*. See **capital letters**

principal or **principle**

Because the words *sound* the same, they are occasionally confused. This sentence straightens it out: 'The *principal* of the college believes in certain *principles* of teaching which were the *principal* things he explained in his speech.'

private parts

This curious expression, even more curious these days when television goes in for 'full frontal exposure', is still used by some doctors and older people for male or female genitals. It would be surprising to hear younger people use it.

privatization and **privatize**

Government policy since the 1980s has brought these words into frequent use. *Privatization* is the opposite of nationalization.

process

How did politicians and trade unions ever manage without this word? Pay-bargaining has become the pay-bargaining *process*, negotiating – the negotiating *process*, talking about peace – the peace *process*, discussion – the discussion *process*. Why not give up making love for the *love-making process*?

processed

Where food is concerned, *processed* is taking on negative connotations, implying the use of chemical additives, although a *food-processor* is simply a machine for chopping up vegetables, etc.

prognosis or **diagnosis**
See **diagnosis**

program or **programme**

In the UK, we use *program* for anything to do with computers, and *programme* at all other times. In the US, it is *program* for all uses.

pronunciation

Pronunciation varies more than any other aspect of English. After all, the slightest change in the way we move the organs of speech changes the sound that comes out. Lloyd James, the expert on phonetics who used to advise the BBC, said, 'Speech is a jumble of noises and rhythms and tunes, whereas the printed page is what it is ....' Don't worry too much if you are unsure about how to pronounce a word. Even Robert Burchfield, who was chief editor of *Oxford English Dictionaries*, admits there's at least one word he pronounces differently every time he says it. Listen carefully to news programmes on TV and radio, because announcers always try to be careful, even if only to prevent other people thumping them for making mistakes. See **accents** and **class language**

Every time an Englishman opens his mouth another Englishman despises him.

George Bernard Shaw, Preface to *Pygmalion*

prophecy or **prophesy**

When we *prophesy* that something will happen we make a *prophecy*.

proportional representation

We hear more and more in the UK about this electoral principle. It is a system under which seats in Parliament would no longer depend on winning seats in constituencies but would be allocated in proportion to the number of votes cast nationally for each party.

proposition

This word has taken on many different meanings, which are only vaguely connected with its original meaning of a proposal. There are *commercial propositions*, *tough propositions*, *paying propositions*, *difficult propositions*, *strange propositions* and several other kinds as well. In

January 1985, a BBC newscaster used *proposition* in another way, when he said that 'Margaret Thatcher was *propositioned* by some dignitary in Edinburgh.' When a man *propositions* a woman, or the other way round, it means only one thing – 'Shall we go to bed together?'

protagonist

Because it sounds like the opposite of 'antagonist', *protagonist* is often mistakenly used to mean someone who supports something: 'She is a *protagonist* of women's rights.' This may be criticized as wrong usage, which it is**. A *protagonist* is the leading character in a drama, film, novel, or in any movement. Hamlet is the *protagonist* in Shakespeare's play, someone could be the *protagonist* of the anti-nuclear lobby.

proved or **proven**

You can say that something has been *proved* or *proven*, although *proved* is the more usual way of saying it, except in Scotland where courts have the right to deliver a verdict 'Not proven' as a third alternative to 'Guilty' or 'Not guilty'.

provided or **providing**

Either is acceptable: 'I can come *provided* (or *providing*) you can pay my fare.' But unless you feel strongly about it, use *provided*, which is considered preferable.

psyche†

Some people are uneasy about using the word 'soul' and, because it has a scientific ring to it, *psyche* is an alternative word to describe what Jung called 'the inmost mystery of life'. *Psyche* is indefinable. It is individual to each person, the essential quality of someone. Pron: 'SYEkee'.

psycho words†

Psycho words proliferate and there are now at least a hundred in English. Some, such as *psychometrics* and *psychosexual*, belong to specialized branches of psychology. Others, especially the word *psychological* itself, are used and misused in a confusion of meanings and non-meanings. A *psychiatrist* always has a specific meaning – a qualified medical practitioner who treats patients suffering from mental disorders. But a psychologist is a much looser term, used for anyone, usually with a degree in psychology, who studies how the mind works. *Psychologists* carry out research or apply their knowledge in industry or advertising, and may also work in hospitals.

The psychiatrist, Dr Sophia Hartland, considers psychotherapy a broad term, covering many different forms of helping patients to overcome mental and emotional difficulties. *Psychotherapy*, she adds, uses listening and talking a great deal, as well as other techniques, but excludes drugs or surgery. *Psychoanalysis* is one example. A *psychotherapist* may be a qualified doctor or may have trained in other ways, without being medically qualified.

I always think of psychology as encompassing the whole of the psyche, and that includes philosophy and theology and many other things besides. For underlying all philosophies and all religions are the facts of the human soul, which may ultimately be the arbiters of truth and error.

C.G. Jung, *The Structure and Dynamics of the Psyche*

psycholinguistics†

The traditional study of words and their meanings is founded on etymology, which is the origin of words and how they have passed into the language. It leaves out something far more important, which is how words affect us and how we react to them. *Psycholinguistics* is the study of the way words interrelate with our minds and emotions. It is hardly recognized in universities but, whether we like it or not, whenever we are reading or listening, writing or speaking, we are involved in *psycholinguistics*: we are being affected and are affecting others, not only by what the words are saying but by their emotional charge.

psychosomatic

The interrelation between the mind and the body. It is used most commonly about illnesses that are brought on or aggravated by mental stress. There is a medical school of thought that believes that most diseases are 'all in the mind'.

punctuation

Reading books on *punctuation* can be like reading books on driving a car: it is not all that much help when you find yourself doing it. The different stops (, ; : .) are there to divide up the flow of words into units of meaning, and the only purpose is to help the reader to take in written language more easily. Sometimes a simple *comma* can make all the difference: 'When it was time to eat knives and forks were put on the table.' Slip in a *comma* after 'eat' and you'll see what I mean. The style generally now is to use fewer commas and more full stops – sentences are shorter in keeping with the faster pace of life. Many people never use a *semi-colon* (;), a less final way of ending a sentence than a full stop; and *colons* (:), almost full stops but not quite, are even less used. Why not try them out occasionally, to see how they feel? A semi-colon (;) has a touch of class about it, and a colon (:) an air of authority. In the end punctuation is more a matter of taste and commonsense than rules. See **dashes**

Stokowski wrote something on his programme and passed it across the dinner-table to the beautiful Rumanian violinist. She was confounded by the sight of one large solitary question mark.

She sent back her reply, from a girl of twenty to a magnificent man of ninety – an exclamation mark.

John Georgiadis, BBC Radio

punk

Punks in the UK demonstrated their rejection of established society by wild hairstyles, outlandish clothes and listening to *punk* rock. Sometimes this violent protest is little more than a fashion, and some punks can be surprisingly gentle people. It would date you to use punk now, as both the word and the style are on the shelf. In America, *punk* is used for someone who is worthless, a write-off, a 'no-good-nik'.

pussy

Concise Oxford and *Longman* dictionaries include this slang word, dating back to the 17th century at least, for a woman's genitals, but call it 'vulgar'. That's as may be, but some women in the UK and the US find *pussy*, used in this sense, quite a friendly word, perhaps because of 'pussycat'. Not all women feel that way, so if you're a man, take care before you use it.

put up with

When Winston Churchill read a sentence that was turned upside down to avoid ending with a preposition, he is said to have made this note in the margin: 'This is the sort of English up with which I will not put.' He was insisting, by exaggeration, that it is good honest English to end a sentence with 'with' 'to' 'for' 'in' or any other preposition. See **prepositions at end of sentences**

pyjamas or **pajamas**

See **pajamas**

Q

quango†

Parliamentarians often talk about *quangos*, but many of the rest of us are uncertain what they are. The letters stand for quasi-autonomous non-governmental organization. Quangos are supposedly independent bodies with statutory powers in the area they operate in. What makes some people uneasy is that the Government controls their finance and appoints the senior officers, so *quango* is often now used in a derogatory way for useless committees.

quantative or **quantitive**

Because of 'qualitative', the wrongly spelled quantative often shows up. Remember 'quantity' which will help you to remember *quantitive*.

quasi-†

You can attach this word, by a hyphen, to many other words to show that something is almost something, but doesn't quite make it. A body can be quasi-governmental (see **quango**), quasi-official, quasi-political. Even the pronunciation hasn't made up its mind: 'KWAHzee' or 'KWAYzeye', whichever you prefer.

queen

Queen is also a slang word for an ageing homosexual who affects a grand lordly manner. It is still used, and at the end of 1984 a book about homosexuals was called – *Queens*. See **gay**

Ernest Thesiger's reply to the question about what it was like to fight at the front in Flanders – 'My dear, the noise! And the people!' – is a perfect example of queenly humour ...

Paul Bailey, *Observer*

queer

At one time queer was the most common word, used in a derogatory way, by heterosexuals about homosexuals. It is used so much less now that it may soon be possible again for *anyone* to feel *queer*, meaning slightly ill. But wait awhile yet, because *queer* is not yet quite out of quarantine. See **gay**

question

If someone says 'That *begs the* question', they may well mean that you have not given them a straight answer. In fact, *beg the question* does not mean that, as so many people suppose. It means to reach a conclusion on the basis of an unproven assumption: 'The plan will fail because of his misguided policies.' That *begs the question*, unless you have proved the policies are misguided. See **leading question**

questionnaire

There is no need to pronounce this the French way: 'kestionNAIRE'. It is more usual now to pronounce the first two syllables the same way as 'question': 'kwestionNAIRE'.

R

racist words

Racialism (pron: 'RAYsherlizm') is prejudice or discrimination against people, usually because of the colour of their skin. A *racialist* is someone prejudiced in this way and also describes any manifestation of *racialism*. *Racism* and *racist* (pron: 'RAYsizm', 'RAYsist') are stronger, more angry variants. Language reflects underlying attitudes and certain words have become highly sensitive. Black people do not want to be called *coloured*. **Negro** is another word that will give offence. *Non-white* is used in the UK occasionally by official organizations, but is better avoided, since in South Africa, it is part of the language of **apartheid**.

At one time, the offensive word *wog* was commonly used by the British about any dark-skinned person, even about almost any foreigner ('Wogs begin at Calais', it was said). *Wog* has almost dropped out of use, except by the most stiff-necked obscurantists and extremists determined to stir up racialism.

The Association of Commonwealth Universities avoids the problem by referring to 'Nigerian students', 'Indian students' and so on. See **apartheid**, **Asian**, **black**, **negro**

Instead of saying 'He is black', many whites would say 'He is a black guy.' This awkwardness was removed by the adoption of 'African-American'. That compound noun is not as stark as 'black'.

William Safire in the *New York Times*

radio

In 1956, according to a BBC survey, more people said 'wireless' than *radio*. That is not true now and 'wireless' now sounds middle-aged, if not elderly. For a while 'transistor' (the name for the electronic conductor that amplifies signals) became the 'in' word for most young people. But now *radio* has moved in as the standard word used by nearly everybody. *Steam radio*, implying that radio is antiquated alongside television, has dropped out since radio has regained so much popularity.

randy

Used for many years about a man who is sexually aroused, it has now become unisex, used by and about women as well. Still rated 'slang' by some dictionaries, it was surprisingly accepted as standard English as long ago as 1976 by the *COD*, although 1984 *LD* called it 'informal'. *Randy* can sound slightly indelicate, in spite of what dictionaries say, so take care where you use it. Not that I can suggest an alternative, except to keep quiet about how you feel.

rapport

Pronounced 'rapPORE' in the UK, 'rapPORT' in the US.

razzle-dazzle and **razzmatazz**†

Interchangeable words to describe a 'showbiz' atmosphere and excitement, such as what happens during US elections. Although considered slang or informal by most dictionaries, *razzle-dazzle* and *razzmatazz* are used at times in serious writing, even in *The Times*.

re or **re-**

Most *re* words do not need a hyphen: *readjust*, *reappraise*, *reassess*, *rework* …. Use a hyphen when the next word begins with *e*: *re-entry*, *re-establish*. And be careful about an occasional confusion of meaning: if you lose your umbrella you want to *recover* it but if it's worn out, it might be worth *re-covering*.

realistic

A common 'cover-up' word. When someone wants something done cheaply, they ask for a *realistic* estimate. When a trade union leader wants a big pay settlement, he asks for a *realistic* offer. *Realistic* means whatever anyone chooses to make it mean, so don't be taken in when someone says 'I can let you have it at a *realistic* price.'

really

Really is a 'filler' word, useful sometimes, at other times meaningless. Its meaning changes according to how you say it. '*Really?*' may equal 'I don't believe what you've just said.' '*Really!*' could mean 'How awful for you.' 'Would you *really* do it?' equals 'Can I rely on you?'

recollect or **remember**

They mean almost the same, but *recollect* implies that you've succeeded after some effort in recalling something, whereas to *remember* something means it came back spontaneously. Subtle maybe, but a useful distinction: 'At last, I have been able to *recollect* what you wanted me to *remember*.'

redbrick

See **Oxbridge**

redundant and **redundancy**

The words mean superfluous, over and above what is required. *Redundancy* is used more now about *people*, which is ominous. Men and women become *redundant* when their jobs disappear because there is no work for them to do or because new technology enables it to be done by fewer workers.

refute

Refute is often wrongly used when politicians are arguing with each other, as an aggressive word meaning to deny something emphatically: 'I *refute* that statement.' *Refute*, when it is properly used, means that conclusive evidence has been produced to show that something is wrong: 'Here are the facts that *refute* that statement.'

... I tell you earnestly and authoritatively ... that you must get into the habit of looking intensely at words and assuring yourself of their meaning, syllable by syllable, nay, letter by letter.

John Ruskin, *Sesame and Lilies*

regretfully or **regrettably**

People may be *regretful* (have feelings of regret) and what they do may be *regrettable* (something to be regretted): 'He *regretfully* decided not to join us' means he felt sorry about it. '*Regrettably* he has decided not to join us' means his decision is regretted by us.

Renaissance or **renaissance**

Some people say 'RENNysance', shown as an alternative pronunciation in dictionaries. But 'reNAYSance' (stress on *second* syllable) is the pronunciation preferred by most scholars. With a capital 'R' it is the name of the creative movement in Europe, starting in the 14th century, that heralded the modern world. With a small 'r' it is used in a more modest way for the *rebirth* (which is what the word means) or revival of ideas or beliefs or a fashion.

renege

When someone goes back on a deal, they *renege*. Pron: 'reNEEG' (to rhyme with 'league') or 'reNAYG' (to rhyme with 'vague').

repel or **repulse**

'Go away – you *repulse* me!' she cried, using the word incorrectly as many people do. *Repulse* is to drive back (as in '*repulsing* an attack') or to rebuff someone by coldness or unkindness ('She was *repulsed* by his unfriendliness'). *Repel* also means to drive away but it can mean to disgust someone. The lady was wrongly linking *repulse* with 'repulsive' which does mean 'disgusting'. She could have cried 'Go away – you *repel* me!' or 'Go away – you're *repulsive*!' and he would have got the message.

reproductive technology†

Reproductive technology is the name for new clinical developments in procreation. These laboratory methods of human reproduction are giving birth, not only to babies but to new words, as well as bringing specialized medical and biological terms into everyday use:

embryology – the aspect of biology dealing with the formation of embryos. There is an embryological laboratory in the famous Bourn Hall procreation clinic in Cambridgeshire.

flushing – the technique by which a woman acts as a living incubator. A fertile woman conceives from sperm taken from an infertile woman's husband. Within a few days the foetus is 'flushed' out and placed within the infertile woman.

sperm banks – there are a number of these in the UK. Semen from donors is deep-frozen and made available to married and, by some clinics, to unmarried women. Semen is also stored for future use by men who are about to have a vasectomy or undergo some other treatment that might result in sterility.

surrogacy – a woman is paid a fee to be fertilized by the sperm from an infertile woman's husband, and to carry and give birth to the baby. The married couple then seek to take legal possession of the child. There are legal and moral aspects of this that many people are uneasy about.

test-tube babies – doctors prefer the term IVF – 'in-vitro fertilization', literally 'in glass', because fertilization is induced in a small glass dish and the resulting embryo transferred to the mother's uterus.

reputable

Because of 'repute', which is stressed on the second syllable ('rePUTE'), it is easy to slip into saying 'rePUTEable'**. Keep the stress on the *first* syllable: 'REPutable'.

research

The tendency, as with some other words, is to bring the stress towards the beginning of the word and say 'REEserch', and this is standard pronunciation in the US. Current dictionaries show this as an alternative pronunciation, although this does not stop a lot of people disliking it and insisting on 'reSERCH' as the correct UK pronunciation.

restaurant

Whether to sound the final 't' or not to sound it, that is the question. *Restaurant* has been used in English since the 19th century, for a place where meals are served. It's as English as Yorkshire pudding, which is why so many people say 'REStoront', with the final 't' sounded. Whatever they say in their private lives, BBC announcers are advised to keep the final 't' silent when they broadcast and say 'REStoranh', with a slight nasal sound in the last syllable. This is the up-market pronunciation.

With notions of 'correctness', as with a number of other warmly held views about spoken and written language, a cool study of past and present uses of English can be a great stabilizer.
Schools Council Project, *The Role of English*

restroom

This is what to ask for in the US if you want a public lavatory. But don't expect to find a bed in it, or even a sofa. See **lavatory** or **loo**

rhetoric†

Rhetoric, the art of using language in speech and writing, used to be a serious subject of study. *Rhetoric* now usually means no more than high-flown political bombast, the same old stuff, signifying nothing much.

rip-off

A colloquial expression that belongs to the age of inflation. A *rip-off* is based on the principle of how much you can charge for something and get away with it. *Rip-off* can apply to meals in restaurants, or to anything else where you feel you have been overcharged and done out of some money.

risk†

Lord Rothschild, in a lecture he called *Risk*, said there is no such thing as a *risk-free* society. The word risk means very little until it is related to the *degree of risk* – is it one in a million or one in ten?

road rage

Drivers have been going berserk for one reason or another ever since the invention of the internal-combustion engine. But *road rage* belongs to our time, a linguistic symbol of our increasingly overcrowded roads. It appeared in print in 1995 and the neat alliteration was an immediate journalistic success. The expression itself has encouraged more drivers to succumb to uncontrolled aggression, beating-up, even killing another driver. *Road rage* is widespread enough for advice on how to deal with it to have found its way into the Highway Code.

robot†

Taken from Karel Capek's play, *R.U.R.*, *robot* was used in English as far back as the 1920s. It became fashionable at one time and then became old hat. With microchip technology, *robot* has come back as one of *the* words of our time. Now when something is made by *robots*, the implication is that it is free from human error. Sir Clive Sinclair, the former computer tycoon, firmly believed that, as the Greeks and the Romans had slaves, the new generation of *robots* will eventually become the slaves of *our* time.

romance

The stress comes on the *second* syllable: 'rerMANS'. 'ROHmans'*, with stress on the first syllable, is perhaps downmarket – except when singing pop songs.

round trip†

In the US, everyone makes *round trips* instead of 'return journeys'. In the UK, people still ask for 'return tickets', but instead of 'return journey', they often say now they are making a round trip, a more logical expression anyway.

royalty

These days you never know when you might have to speak to a member of the royal family. If it's the queen, then always begin with 'Your Majesty'. After that, you can relax and simply say 'ma'am'. Protocol requires us not to ask the queen a question, but in the 21st century it's unlikely that you'd be beheaded for asking 'Would Your Majesty care for a drink?' You can take it easy when speaking to other royals, as in everyday situations it's usually all right simply to use 'Sir' or 'Ma'am'.

S

sadism

See **masochism**

safe sex

This term belongs to the post-AIDS culture, and is used for having sex with a condom.

samurai

Japanese films have made this word known in the West. A *samurai* was a member of the warrior aristocracy in Japan, fiercely arrogant and bound by a strict code of conduct. A samurai can now also mean any Japanese army officer. Plural is same as the singular: *samurai* (usually pron: 'SAMyooreye').

sanction

Sanctions can be imposed as a penalty or as a way of enforcing a law. The word is also used for a formal way of giving permission: 'The Governing Body sanctioned his leave of absence.' Avoid using sanction to mean 'imposing sanctions or a penalty' ('He was *sanctioned* for his absence').

sang or **sung**

'I *sung* a song yesterday' is still good English although the normal form now is 'I sang a song ....' But always 'A song was *sung*.'

sank or **sunk**

'The ship sank', not 'the ship sunk', which is obsolete. But 'the ship was sunk'. The older form *sunken* survives in 'a sunken garden', 'a *sunken* road', '*sunken* treasure'.

Saudi

Huge profits from oil have made some *Saudis* rich beyond imagination. Call them 'SOWdis' *not* 'SAWdis'.

scab

In 1984 *scab* became one of the most abusive words in English, as it was shouted out during the year-long miners' strike, even by children, at anyone who defied the strike call. In those days scab was 'slang', but it has now passed into standard English (*COD* and *LD*).

scan

As well as a number of technical and medical meanings, and the literary meaning of analysing the rhythm of verse, the everyday meaning of *scan* is to look at something intently. But *scan* is often used now to mean the opposite to look through something quickly ('She *scanned* the property ads looking for a flat'). Look out for possible confusion: 'Would you *scan* that report' really means go through it carefully, but for some people it would mean – take a quick look at it.

scarcely

See **hardly**

scenario

Scenario sounds impressive, so in the heady days of Hollywood it became the standard word for the script of a film. Now you are much more likely to hear 'screen-play' in the US and 'filmscript' in the UK. A more recent use of *scenario* is for a sequence of events in the past or forecast for the future: 'This is the *scenario* that led up to the crisis', 'The scenario for what will happen next is ....' *Scenario* is also used, in a pointless way, as an alternative for 'situation': 'Faced with this *scenario*, he had to resign.' Pron: 'seNAHrio' in UK, 'seNAIRrio' in US.

schedule

Pronounced 'SHEDyool' in the UK, 'SKEDyool' in US. 'SKEDyool'** is sometimes heard in the UK but jars on many people.

schlep†

A Yiddish word (from German *schleppen*, to drag) meaning to carry heavy or cumbersome things from one place to another. *Schlep* is familiar idiom in New York, often heard in 'showbiz' circles in the UK and shows up (as informal usage) in *LD*.

Queen Elizabeth will schlep along 95 pieces of baggage on her trip here.

> *New York Post*, 29 September 1957, quoted by Leo Rosten in *The Joys of Yiddish*

schmaltz†

Elevated to standard English by some recent dictionaries, this Yiddish word is curiously listed even in the *Oxford Dictionary for Writers and Editors*. It is a most expressive word for anything, especially music, that is excessively sentimental and cloying. Roughly equivalent to the old slang word 'corny' but much more colourful.

science or technology

Technology has been in English since the early 17th century but in recent years it has become the standard word for *applied science*, an all-embracing word for *science* used in industry and business. *Science* tends to be used now mostly for research and in academic contexts.

Science and *technology* are words of progress, as they have always been, but more than ever before, they are also words of fear and apprehension at the *speed* of that progress.

Scientists are inheriting, they are conquering the earth. If you do not speak their uncouth language, then you will sink to the status of the native yokels when the Normans overran England.

> Dr Bronowski at a congress of the British
> Association, quoted by Brian Foster in
> *The Changing English Language*

A bowl of Scotch Mr. MacTavish?

BROTH

Scotch or Scottish

North of the Border, ever since the late 19th century, they have preferred to call nearly everything *Scottish* ('*Scottish* scenery', '*Scottish* food', etc.). Now *Scottish* is the accepted word to use everywhere. Talk about a *Scotsman*, a *Scotswoman* or the *Scots*. But there is no obligation to ask for *Scottish broth* or *Scottish whisky*, as even the Scots are quite happy to keep Scotch firmly anchored to those words, to say nothing of 'Scotch mist'!

screw

This word has many meanings. Most people know the

slang usage that goes back a hundred years: *screw* – to have sexual intercourse. This is 'vulgar' – a five-letter word among the *four-letter words*, but is used widely this way in the UK and the US; and it is heard on television. According to the book, *The Slanguage of Sex*, the most popular of all Sunday newspapers, famous for reporting sexual scandals, is sometimes called *The News of the Screws* or *The Screws of the World*!

secretary

People, anxious to avoid gabbling and saying 'seketry', sometimes go too far the other way, saying 'sekretairy'. The accepted UK pronunciation is 'SEK-re-try' (*three* syllables). In the US, *four* syllables are standard: 'SEK-retairy'. Women, and not only feminists, can be justifiably angry when a man refers to his *secretary* as 'my girl': 'I'll get *my girl* to see to it.' This is insensitive and out of touch. See **girl**

section or **sector†**

Sector used to be primarily a technical term and *section* the more general expression. But now *sector* has become standard for referring to a *section* of the economy ('the private sector' for example) or of society.

self or **self-**

Self- can be prefixed to many words and nearly always a hyphen should be used: *self-catering, self-composed, self-conscious, self-contained, self-drive, self-fulfilling, self-pity, self-sufficient*, etc.

self-centred or **selfish**

It is unfortunate that these words are sometimes used interchangeably, because there is a valuable distinction. *Selfish* is thinking just of yourself and not giving a damn about others. *Self-centred* is being intelligently aware of yourself, as an individual and in relation to others. But not everyone accepts that difference of meaning.

seminal†

Used in biological contexts to do with semen and reproduction, seminal is often used more widely now to describe something that contains the seeds of future creative development: 'a *seminal* book', '*seminal* ideas', 'a *seminal* speech'.

Semitic

Because of *anti-Semitic* (meaning discrimination against Jews), *Semitic* is sometimes believed to have only one meaning, which is 'Jewish'. But there are other *Semitic* peoples, such as Arabs, Phoenicians, Ethiopians and Assyrians.

sensual or sensuous

Although some people use both these words in much the same way, *sensual* is usually pejorative, implying lustful indulgence in sex or excessive pleasure from food: 'She resented the *sensual* way he sized up her body.' *Sensuous* is a harmless word for enjoying something with one's senses: 'She loved the *sensuous* pleasure of swimming in a warm sea.' This is a distinction worth preserving.

serviette

Words, like clothes, go out of fashion and for some perverse reason this elegant word is decidedly downmarket. The 'best' people say 'napkin'.

sewed or sewn

The older form *sewn* is often used ('It is *sewn* by hand') and preferred by tailors. *Sewed* is also correct.

sexist language

The fuss that is made about words such as 'chairman', 'spokesman', 'mankind', etc. and the insistence, by some, on unisex forms (*chairperson*, *spokesperson*, *humankind*, etc.) reflect a much deeper social problem. Despite equal pay legislation, women generally still earn less than men, they're grossly under-represented in the professions, they take on most of the clerical and welfare work, and there are still far fewer women MPs than men. Feminists, and other women too, hope to change underlying attitudes by changing the words that reflect them. Linguistic habits are among the most difficult of all to shift and even women are divided, some feeling passionately about it, others finding the whole feminist issue exaggerated. But the same was also true of the struggle, earlier this century, for votes for women. In the 21st century, both women and men should at least be aware of words and expressions that could degrade or belittle women. See **girl** and **Ms**

If you put things firmly they say you're headmistressy … but they never call a man headmastery.

Margaret Thatcher

sexology†

The *Shorter Oxford Dictionary* used to include this word as an afterthought, in the addenda at the back. Thanks to Alfred Kinsey, Masters and Johnson and all the others who have probed and pried into what were once 'dirty

dark secrets', no dictionary now could leave out *sexology*. *Sexologists* carry out exhaustive research into what goes on between women and men in bed. Other *sexologists* treat people with sexual hang-ups and others pontificate in books on how to 'do it'. A writer once called sex the 'ever-interesting topic', which makes *sexology* for many people the most fascinating of all *-ologies*.

Graduates could boast a BSc in Sexology after taking thirty courses from a total of thirty-seven course options including Personal Maturation I & II (which require experiments with sensitization, non-verbal interaction, bioenergetics, and transcendental meditation), Sexopathology, Ethnosexology, Sex and Civilizations, in all a wonderful brew of biology, psychiatry, psychology, psychoanalysis, sociology, criminology, anthropology, education and philosophy.

Germaine Greer, Sex and Destiny

sexy

One authority gives 1928 as the year when *sexy* first appeared in English. Another scholar found it in a letter written in 1925. Either way, it's a useful word, which *LD* considers 'informal' but Oxford dictionaries rate as standard English. Another dictionary defines 'sexy' as 'immoderately concerned with sex', with a later secondary meaning 'to be sexually attractive to an immoderate degree'. Both definitions seem uptight and many people feel relaxed about using sexy in a friendly, even admiring way, without any pejorative suggestion.

shall or will

Nearly everyone has been taught something about this at school and a few still follow the copybook rules meticulously. The English are taught: 1. I/we *shall*, you/he/she/it *will* = simple future: 'I *shall* be leaving tomorrow', 'I hope it *will* be ready on time.' 2. I/we *will*, you/he etc. *shall* = intention or determination: 'I *will* succeed whatever happens', 'You *shall* do it, whatever you say.' But in Scotland, Ireland and the US, 'I will' is normal usage for the simple future; and in his famous wartime speech of defiance, Churchill used 'we shall' not to express simple future but the utmost determination: 'We *shall* fight in the fields and in the streets, we *shall* fight in the hills; we *shall* never surrender.'

It is a confusing picture and you can go out of your mind trying to sort it out. The best advice I can give is this: if you like the standard rules about *shall* and *will*, keep to them. Otherwise use whichever comes naturally, remembering that the tendency now is for *will* to replace *shall* in all cases, especially in spoken English. To some people, 'I shall' even sounds rather old-fashioned. I am already preparing to be attacked for that advice, but it is the way some good writers and speakers deal with *shall* and *will*. Occasionally you can side-step the problem with I'll, she'll, etc. See **contracted forms**

she or **he**

See **he**

sheikh

You never know when you might meet one these days, so remember the pronunciation: 'shake'. In the US, 'sheek' is more usual.

sheila†

Friendly slang in Australia and New Zealand for a girl or a young woman and now occasionally heard in the UK as well.

ship or **boat**

See **boat**

shirt

See **blouse**

shit**

Though it has been heard in talks on the BBC, *shit* remains an indecent word for most people. Your doctor may call it 'stool'; if you squelch in some on the pavement, you can say 'dog mess' and perhaps that covers most of the times you need a 'polite' alternative. See **four-letter words** and **piss**

should or **would**

The basic rule used to be: I/we *should*, you/she/he/it *would*. But this is often ignored now. *Plain Words*, the guide to English written for civil servants, quotes even a Professor of Poetry using *would* and *should* interchangeably, which has become almost standard practice. *Should* can be used, in addition, to mean 'ought to': 'You *should* leave early to avoid the rush hour.'

showed or **shown**

'It was *showed* to her' or 'It was *shown* …'? Dictionaries accept both but shown is preferable. The spellings 'shew', 'shewn' are archaic and would be affected now.

simplistic†

It derives from 'simple' but it does not mean the same, which is the way some people use it. *Simplistic* always carries with it the pejorative meaning of over-simplified, naïve or even downright stupid.

sixth

It's sloppy to drop the -s- sound and say 'sikth'. Pron: 'siksth'.

slander or **libel**

See **libel**

slang

Slang, at its best, keeps English alive by injections of new, rich and colourful words, which through films and television are soon spread round the English-speaking world. But a good deal of *slang* is junk language and doesn't deserve to survive. *Slang* that is all right in one place can be all wrong in another – Professor Randolph Quirk offers this example: 'Hi, John: I'm just phoning to say your sister has croaked.'

If you use too much *slang* it will sound sloppy: if you never use *slang* you will sound stuffy. Above all, never give up the idea of using a word or an expression because you're afraid it's *slang* – look it up and you may find it was coined by Shakespeare.

Slang is the one stream of poetry that is constantly flowing.
G.K. Chesterton

sleep

The most euphemistic way to say that a man and a woman are having sexual relations is to say they *sleep together*. It is so polite that even the 1982 *COD* admitted the usage as standard English (although 'informal' in *LD*). It has been in use for donkey's years and is as current as ever now. To *sleep around*, meaning to be sexually promiscuous, is slang and, unfair though it is, tends to be used more about women than men.

Sloane Ranger

The profile of a *Sloane Ranger* went something like this: tall, angular, two labradors on a lead, a Range Rover (with children's 'hard hats' on the back seat), living within walking or easy taxi distance of Sloane Street and King's Road in London, and with an account at *Peter Jones* and *Harrods*. The concept started in 1982 with *The Sloane Ranger Handbook* (written by Anne Barr and Peter York) and the phrase stuck as a description of affluent self-assured people whose idea of the Third World was Bermuda and the Antilles. Although used mostly about women, there were male *Sloane Rangers* too: the magazine *Harpers and Queen* advertised 'The official *Sloane Ranger* men's shirt', using as a model a well set-up man. But the term *Sloane Ranger* has become faded and nostalgic, although you still hear it.

smelled or **smelt**

Both are right but *smelt* is the usual form in the UK and *smelled* in the US.

sociable or **social**

A person can be *sociable*, that is enjoying being with other people; an organization, principle, problem, etc. can be *social*, that is relating to society: '*social* club', '*social* worker', etc. But the distinction is becoming blurred and a friendly gregarious person is sometimes described as 'very social'.

Socialist or **socialist**

A *Socialist* (capital S) is a member of a socialist political party and a *socialist* (small s) is anyone who believes in the principles of socialism.

sociology

Pron: 'sohseeOLogee' or 'sohsheeOLogee'. Although this fashionable science is concerned with human beings in society, the language used by sociologists is becoming ever more remote, obscured by jargon such as 'residential structures' (houses), 'adult males and females in the roles of parents' (fathers and mothers). See **jargon**

solidarity

Solidarity means the mutual dependence of people on one another, without political implications. But since September 1980, when the Committee for the Defence of Workers in Poland joined with Polish trade unions under the name *Solidarity*, the word has become synonymous with working or deprived people supporting each other against management and the State. That is what *SOLIDARITY* means when you see it defiantly spraygunned on walls anywhere in the world.

solvent abuse

The formal expression for 'glue-sniffing', the dangerous and addictive practice that, tragically, some young people go in for to induce a hallucinogenic state, as a cheap alternative to drugs.

somebody or someone

See **everybody**

some time or sometime

It nearly always appears now as one word but there is a difference if you want to preserve it. *Sometime* means any time and *some time* means a certain period of time: 'I'll arrive *sometime* on Monday', 'It is *some time* since she has seen him.'

son-in-laws or sons-in-laws

See **daughter-in-laws**

sophisticated

Some purists still insist on using this word only in its original pejorative sense of devious, not pure or genuine, and this was still the primary meaning shown in 1959 *Shorter Oxford Dictionary*. But now nearly everyone uses *sophisticated*, usually with no negative implication, to mean worldly, urbane, socially poised: 'Although she is young, he was impressed by her *sophisticated* manner.' It is also used about something intellectual or subtle ('a *sophisticated* argument') or about something technologically advanced ('a *sophisticated* piece of equipment'). These uses are established.

south

See **north, south, east** and **west**

Soviet

The pronunciation 'SOHviette' is recommended to BBC

announcers but some of them still say 'SOVviette' (*o* as in
'sock'). Both pronunciations are perfectly all right. In any
case, the word now belongs to history.

space travel

The vocabulary of *space travel*, as remarked on by Sir
Bruce Fraser in *Plain Words*, is generally refreshingly simple: *Spacemen* or *spacewomen* wearing *spacesuits* are
blasted-off in a *spaceship*, experience *weightlessness* while
they set up *space stations* before returning to earth for a
splash-down. Computer science and other new techno-
logies, please copy! See **astronaut**

spelled or **spelt**

See **smelled** or **smelt**

spelling

English spelling is no joke, even for the English; foreign-
ers tear their hair out. The US has gone some way
towards rationalizing spelling (*-or* for *-our, traveling,
traveled* for *travelling, travelled* and so on), but even the
most modest reforms arouse great hostility in the UK. We
are stuck with our difficult spelling and there are enough
exceptions to every rule to make it hardly worth learning
any rule, except one: when in doubt, look it up in a dictionary.

> *Suzy, though you've studied so,*
> *You must take one final blow.*
> *Is the proper rhyme for tough*
> *Though, through, plough, cough, or enough?*
> *Hiccough has the sound of cup.*
> *Suzy, better give it up*!
>> Part of a verse devised to help multinational
>> personnel of NATO learn English (quoted
>> by Willard R. Espy in *Words at Play*)

sperm bank

See **reproductive technology**

spilled or **spilt**

See **smelled** or **smelt**

spin-off†

Useful expression to describe a by-product or secondary
benefit, often unexpected, derived from something

planned for an altogether different purpose. A journalist is flying to Paris to report on fashion shows and on the plane she meets a man whom she subsequently marries. That's a *spin-off*! A popular children's TV programme makes even more money from the *spin-off* of toys being sold, based on characters in the programme.

spinster

This cold word for a woman who has never married, which was often used to imply unwanted and 'on the shelf', has almost dropped out of use. That's no loss.

split infinitive

The longest-running controversy in English grammar and still alive and kicking. For the record, an *infinitive* is *to* followed by a verb: 'to walk', 'to consider', 'to love', etc. When another word comes between to and the verb ('to *carefully* consider', 'to *passionately* love'), that is a *split infinitive*, which to some people is still a crime: 'Listening to the 8 o'clock news on the wireless this morning, I was appalled to hear that two infinitives had been split within three minutes of each other' (letter to the BBC). The famous *Bullock Report* on the teaching of English (1975) dismissed the whole business as one of the rules 'invented quite arbitrarily by grammarians in the 18th and 19th

The question is whether to sort of split them or to really seriously and irrevocably split them.

centuries'. Yet many writers on English are uneasy about giving the green light to split infinitives. In *Plain Words*, Sir Bruce Fraser (whose attitude towards English usage is balanced and reasonable) advises against *splitting* 'not because you care about the taboo, but because you care about your reputation with readers'. That sums it up. If you don't want to upset anyone, you will avoid *split infinitives*; if you care more about writing good clear English, you will use words where they fall most natural-ly, whether they split an infinitive or not.

There is a busybody on your staff who devotes a lot of time to chasing split infinitives. Every good literary craftsman splits his infinitives when the sense demands it. I call for the immediate dismissal of this pedant. It is of no consequence whether he decides to go quickly, or quickly to go, or to quickly go. The important thing is that he should go at once.
Bernard Shaw, letter to *The Times* (1907)

spoiled or **spoilt**
See **smelled** or **smelt**
spokesperson
A unisex word that still sounds awkward, although it is heard regularly on the BBC and used in newspapers. See **sexist language**
spoonfuls or **spoonsful**
It will taste the same whether you add two *spoonfuls* or two *spoonsful* and *LD* gives you the choice. *Spoonfuls* is easier to say and sounds more natural.
St
See **abbreviations**
standard English
When books refer to *standard English*, they mean English that is considered correct by most educated people for writing and speaking, in nearly all situations. The prob-lem is there is no final authority on where slang and colloquial language end and *standard English* begins. About many words and expressions, most people agree. About others, even good dictionaries take different views on whether a word or a phrase is slang or colloquial, or *standard English*, or sometimes whether it is English at

all. That's why, in this book, it seems more reasonable to avoid laying down the law, by spelling *standard* with a small s – to suggest a generally accepted standard of educated usage, not an absolute fixed standard that everyone agrees with.

Star Wars

In 1977, George Lucas directed *Star Wars*, one of the most successful films ever made. In the 1980s, reality caught up with science fiction and *Star Wars* passed into English (although not yet shown in all dictionaries) as the standard phrase for strategic defence systems in outer space, designed to counteract missiles. US defence secretaries use it freely.

States or US or America

On both sides of the Atlantic, the *States* is commonly used for the *United States of America*. In writing, *US* is more formal, but in speech *US* seems colloquial and it's better to say the *United States*. *America* is often used as a synonym for the US, which is all right provided the context makes it clear you do not also mean Canada and the countries of Central and South America.

stationary or stationery

We all learn the difference at school but some people still have to think about it. Think of all the 'e's in 'envelope' and you will remember that paper, pens, postcards, envelopes, etc. are *stationEry*.

status

The alternative pronunciations 'STAYtus' and 'STATTtus' are approved by *LD* but some dictionaries list 'STAYtus' as the *only* acceptable way to say it.

still lifes or still lives

A cat has nine *lives* but in the art world the plural of *still life* is always *still lifes*.

stop off and stop over

Although some people still object to them as Americanisms, these expressions have become standard English in the UK. And they are useful because *stop off* and *stop over* imply a stop at an *intermediate* point in a journey (*stop over* suggesting staying at least overnight), whereas to *stop* somewhere could mean the end of the journey.

strategy or **tactics**

Easy to confuse. *Strategy* is broad policy, medium to long term planning. *Tactics* are day-to-day ways of achieving the long term plan. *Strategy* is where you are going: *tactics* are how you get there.

strength

It is preferable to sound the -g-, rather than saying 'strenth'.

stress

Stress has several meanings but the most common way the word is used now is for the mental and physical *stress* of competing in business and professional work. *Stress*, in this sense, has become a killer, leading to coronaries, alcoholism and other forms of physical and nervous breakdowns. *Stress* now has a new and sinister meaning.

style

We recognize *style* in using language, when we hear it or read it, but it doesn't follow that we can reproduce it ourselves. An awareness of words is the first requirement and I hope this book helps. After that, it is work, the willingness to write and rewrite, which has always been the hallmark of style in the use of words.

The other meaning of *style* is more indefinable. It is something about the way someone dresses, or their manner, or how they appear to others as human beings. The need for *style* in that last sense, is now considered of first importance, for as George-Louis de Buffon maintained, '*Style* is the man himself.'

I am not pleased when people tell me I have a nice style. I just try to write as clearly as I can to let those thoughts appear on the page. I don't want style to stand out, I don't want the words to get in the way.

V.S. Naipaul, winner of the 2001
Nobel Prize for Literature

subconscious or **unconscious**

In psychology both words refer to that part of the mind we are not usually aware of but which manifests itself in dreams and influences behaviour. The *unconscious*, used by Freud and especially by Jung, has become the more

usual word and subconscious is not heard much now. See
Freudian slip

subnormal or **abnormal**

See **abnormal**

summary or **outline**

See **outline**

super or **super-**

Some people (for whom so many things are *Super*!') may
he surprised to learn that *super* has been around in
English since the 14th century. Much later, in 1903,
Bernard Shaw started something with his play *Man and
Superman*. It has led to a never-ending flow of new
supers: *supermarket*, *superpower*, *supersonic*, *superego*,
supergrass, *supertanker* and many more, culminating in
Andrew Lloyd Webber's *Jesus Christ – Superstar*.
Inevitably *super* has become a favourite of advertising
agencies – the *super-soft* option for copywriters! Most
super words do not take a hyphen – see examples above.

supercede or **supersede**

If you have been spelling it *supercede*, I sympathize – I did
for years. But the right spelling, take it or leave it, is
supersede and dictionaries do *not* allow *supercede*.

surrogacy†

See **reproductive technology**

surveillance

The hang-up for anyone who knows French is whether to
pronounce the -ll-. You should: 'surVAYLlance'.

swam or **swum**

This way round: 'I have *swum* a long way', 'I *swam*
yesterday.'

sympathetic†

The primary meaning remains showing compassion for
someone's suffering. But now even the most conservative
dictionaries accept as standard English the secondary
meaning – likeable and appealing. This is the way the
French use *sympathique*, the Italians *simpatico* and the
Germans *sympatisch*: about a person, a restaurant, a film,
about anything or anyone they find warm and agreeable.
Unsympathetic can be used in the opposite sense for anything or anyone cold and off-putting. See **empathy** or
sympathy

syndrome†

A fashionable word sometimes misused as in 'She's suffering from an anxiety *syndrome*.' In medicine, a *syndrome* is not a disease but a complex of symptoms pertaining to a particular malfunction. So you cannot 'suffer from a syndrome'. The proper extended use of the word is useful to express a range of manifestations coming from a single cause: 'it's all part of the permissiveness syndrome', meaning different ways in which permissiveness is expressed in society.

Be sure that you go to the author to get at his *meaning, not to find yours.*

John Ruskin, *Sesame and Lilies*

T

table

For years we have 'put our cards on the table' when we explain exactly where we stand over anything; we have 'turned the tables' (an expression from the game of chess for when the board is reversed) on someone when we change what was to their advantage to *our* advantage. When we table something, we put it on the agenda for discussion (note: to *table* something in the US, in parliamentary usage, is to remove it temporarily or indefinitely from further consideration). Another usage has become fashionable: governments, trade unions, corporations no longer negotiate – they 'sit round the negotiating table', and instead of pay settlements being agreed, management and unions 'go to the bargaining table'. *Table* is now used as an evocative image in any kind of horse-trading situation.

tablet or **pill**

See **pill**

tactics or **strategy**

See **strategy**

tarif** or **tariff**

Always two fs: *tariff*.

Hi Julian. Meet the tart!

tart

In the 19th century this was generally an endearing slang word for a prostitute, probably deriving from 'sweetheart'. It has since become derogatory and abusive, used about a woman who is promiscuous or sexually provocative. To 'get *tarted* up' or to '*tart* something up', meaning to make yourself or something attractive, are still friendly harmless slang expressions.

> *The family had quite a start,*
> *When Auntie Jane became a tart.*
> *But blood is blood and race is race;*
> *And so to mitigate disgrace,*
> *They bought her a most expensive beat –*
> *From Asprey's down to Oxford Street.*
>
> Anonymous 19th-century verse

Tass
The word was formed from the initials of the Russian name for the former Soviet news agency, the main source of all official news from the old USSR.

tautology
Tautology is the grammarian's term for unnecessary words that add nothing but padding: '*unfilled* vacancy', '*past* history', '*recent* news', '*final* upshot'. Some unnecessary words do add a useful emphasis or are evocative, and Eric Partridge was too severe when he wrote off as *tautology* expressions such as: 'appear *on the scene*', 'hurry *up*', '*just* recently' and even 'twice *over*'. See **pleonasm** and **verbosity**

tax avoidance or **tax evasion**†
We are entitled to go in for as much *tax avoidance* as we can, because that covers any *legal* way of reducing the amount of tax we pay, such as claiming all deductions and allowances. *Tax evasion* is something else: it is deliberately giving false information in order to pay less tax. *Tax avoidance* is honest: *tax evasion* is illegal.

tax exile
A *tax exile* is someone, usually with a high income, who chooses to live in another country where there is a low level of taxation. Such countries are called *tax havens*.

teach-in†
Imported in the 1960s from the campuses of American universities, where it used to be just another expression

for a class or seminar. It is now used in the US and in the UK for a long session of lectures or discussions, usually on a controversial issue, and also for an informal gathering of people who want to widen their knowledge about something through discussion and the exchange of ideas. *Teach-in* sometimes carries with it a suggestion of rebellion or defiance.

technology

See **science**

teenager

When the American word *teenager* crossed the Atlantic, it filled a real linguistic need. The alternative word, 'adolescent', suggests young people in transition between childhood and adulthood: *teenager* recognizes a politically conscious group able to make its own demands on society, which is a fact of life in the 21st century.

telephone

See **phone**

television or **TV** or **telly**

'I saw it on TV' is as much standard English now as 'I saw it on television.' But 'I saw it on the telly' is perhaps down-market. 'I saw it on the box', at one time the most common expression, is still used but is dated.

temporarily

It's easier to put the stress on the *third* syllable: 'temperRERily'* but this is considered wrong by people. The approved pronunciation is to stress the *first* syllable: 'TEMpererily'.

terrorist

Whether someone is a *terrorist* can depend on which side you're on. In the Lebanon, the Israelis called the guerilla forces *terrorists* – the Lebanese called them 'resistance fighters'. See **guerilla**

test-tube babies

See **reproductive technology**

than I or **than me***

Which is good English: 'She is richer *than I*' or 'She is richer *than me*'? The same question applies to *than he* and *than him*. The argument centres round the grammatical function of the word *than*. There are many examples among good writers and speakers of *than me* and *than him* and Eric Partridge, a conservative scholar, comes out in favour of *than me*. Other grammarians insist on *than I* and *than he*. The game is hardly worth the candle and perhaps we should use whichever comes naturally. For most of us that will be *than me* and *than him*: 'She is taller *than me*', 'She arrived earlier *than him*.' If you prefer *than I*, etc., then it's often better to complete the sentence: 'She is taller than I am', 'She arrived earlier than he did.' Otherwise it can sound stilted. In some sentences, look out for the risk of confusion: 'She loves him more than me' could mean 'She loves him more than she loves me' or 'She loves him more than I love him.' In such cases the best thing is to spell it out and say what you mean.

that

So often we're not sure whether to put *that* in or leave it out: 'I believe *that* the book *that* she has written is *that* one.' The first two *thats* could be deleted and the sentence remains good English and perfectly clear: 'I believe the book she has written is *that* one.' When *that* is unnecessary for the sense or the sound, you can leave it out, unless you want to sound formal or dignified.

that or **which** or **who**

A few grammarians maintain there is a difference in meaning between: 'White wine *that* is dry goes well with fish' and 'White wine *which* is dry goes well with fish.' Since both sentences mean the same to so many people, there is little point in insisting on a distinction between *that* and *which*. The same applies to: 'Please explain it again to the women *that* came late' and '... the women *who* came late'. Both sentences are good English, although 'the women who' sounds more natural.

On *that or which or who*, Sir Bruce Fraser in *Plain Words* gives short sharp advice – *Don't fuss*. But a few people will go on fussing about it and expect you to do the same.

theirs or **their's**

Never *their's****.

therefore

At one time *therefore* was always preceded and followed by a *comma*: 'I consider, therefore, that ....' There is usually no need to put *commas* in these days and they do have the effect of making *therefore* seem rather heavy-going.

they or he

Which is correct: 'If anyone believes that, *he* would be wrong' or '... *they* would be wrong'? See **everybody**

Third World†

This signified those countries of Africa, Asia and Latin America not politically aligned with either the Communist or the Capitalist countries, which were considered as two worlds apart. The *Third World* (initial capitals are not always used) is now used increasingly to mean the under-developed underprivileged countries of the world.

though or although

See **although**

till or until

Interchangeable.

tit*

Dictionaries can be funny about words. *LD* regards *tit* as standard English for a nipple, but slang for a woman's breast. The latest *COD* writes down *tit* as coarse slang for a woman's breast. The word is natural enough to most of us and few people would think of it as vulgar. *Tit* is also a slang word for someone who is irritating and stupid ('He's making a tit of himself').

Lexicographer: a writer of dictionaries, a harmless drudge.
Samuel Johnson, *Dictionary of the English
Language* (1755)

titivate or titillate

They do not mean the same, as some people believe. *Titivate* is standard English for the slang expression 'to tart something up'. *Titillate* means to excite someone though not very much, and is often used for mild sexual stimulation, more teasing than torrid.

to

Whatever anyone may say, 'What are you referring *to*?' is perfectly good English. See **prepositions at end of sentences**

toilet or lavatory or loo

See **lavatory**

ton or tonne

Ton represents various units of weight, the most common

of which is 20 hundredweight (2,240 pounds). *Tonne* is a metric measurement and equals 1,000 kilograms (approx. 2,205 pounds) which is not all that much different from a standard *ton*. Both *ton* and *tonne* are pronounced the same and if you need to indicate which is which in speech, simply refer to *tons* or *metric tonnes*.

topless

Perhaps there's still something nudge-nudge, wink-wink about this word, thanks to *topless* waitresses in *topless* bars. But it's the only word we use now on beaches, for women wearing bikini bottoms only.

total of

A total of 14 men *is* or *are*? It is the same rule as for **number of** (see entry).

toward or **towards**

Either: *towards* is more usual in the UK and *toward* in the US. 'Tords' (one syllable) used to be the 'in' way of saying it and a few people still keep to that. But 'to-wards' (two syllables and sounding the 'w') is standard now.

trade-off†

Not in all dictionaries yet, although you hear it at board meetings and read it in business magazines. A *trade-off* is a commercial or realistic balance between one consideration and another. If you made a car as safe as technology could make possible, it would cost too much for most people to buy. So you make it as safe as you can consistent with selling it at a competitive price. There's a *trade-off* between safety and competitiveness.

trade union or **trades union**

Both forms exist. Some older trade-unionists seem to prefer *trades union* but *trade union* (plural: *trade unions*) is more usual now, except for *Trades Union Congress* (TUC). Note: *trade union* (no hyphen), *trade-unionism* and *trade-unionist* (usually with a hyphen).

trait

'Tray' is the preferred pronunciation. Some people look down on 'trait' as a vulgarism, although this is the pronunciation shown first in the *LD* and is standard in America.

tranquillizer

The standard word now for drugs that relieve anxiety. Sex can also be a *tranquillizer* and so can food, which has been called 'the oldest *tranquillizer* in the world'.

trans or **trans-**

Nearly all *trans* words appear as *one* word: *transatlantic, transcontinental, transnational, transoceanic, transsexual* ....

transcendental†

It was *Transcendental Meditation* (known as *TM*), a kind of brand name for a particular technique of meditation, that brought *transcendental* into popular use. Apart from contexts in academic philosophy, the word connotes something beyond ordinary human experience, a surpassing of the ego and attachment to this life. The essential block to understanding the real meaning of *transcendental* is the impossibility of knowing unless you have experienced it. See **nirvana**

transferable

Most dictionaries allow the option of putting the stress on the *first* syllable or the *second*. Nevertheless the preferred pronunciation is 'TRANSferable' (rather than 'transFERable').

transistor

See **radio**

transpire

When something *transpires*, it becomes known: 'It *transpired* that he had been deceiving her for years.' Some books on English condemn the 'common error' of using transpire to mean 'to happen': 'Let's see what *transpires* when they meet.' This 'common error' has existed in English for at least 150 years and well-known writers, including Dickens, have used *transpire* in this way. Dictionaries have grudgingly come round to showing 'to happen' or 'to occur' as one of the meanings of *transpire*, although a few people still consider this unacceptable. Often the 'misuse' of a word eventually passes into standard English and the shouting dies away. This has almost happened with *transpire*.

transsexual

A *transsexual* is not the same as a homosexual or a lesbian. *Transsexuality* is when a man or a woman has an irresistible psychological need to belong to the other sex, driving them sometimes to undergo a surgical operation.

trattoria†

This Italian word for a simple eating place has been used in English since the 1830s. In the last few years, so many Italian restaurants and spaghetti-houses have opened up, that *trattoria* (and the slang abbreviation *tratt*) has become familiar. A *trattoria* is properly a simple restaurant but don't bank on that now – some *tratts* are fashionable and expensive. Pron: 'tratterREEer'.

travelled and **traveller**

Spelt *traveled* and *traveler* in America.

trip†

Not all dictionaries have given good coverage to extended meanings of *trip*. Starting with its basic meaning of a short journey ('a *trip* to the seaside'), other interesting usages have developed. To *take a trip* can mean using hallucinogenic drugs to be transported into a visionary experience. An *ego-trip* is a self-indulgent exercise, which could be writing a book, making a film, or almost anything else. To go on *a nostalgia trip* is to wallow in sentimentality. A *bad trip* is a highly disturbing emotional experience and is also associated with a bad experience from drugs. *Trip* has proved a useful word in recent years and we shall hear more of it.

try and or **try to**

For many years *try and* was condemned as ungrammatical and we had to *try to* avoid it all the time. It is now usual to accept that *try and* is all right when we're talking, but some people avoid it in writing. Spoken English is all the time influencing written English, and *try and* is so common in conversation that it's not surprising that it also appears in serious writing. *Try and* is almost standard usage but you would avoid criticism if you *try to* avoid it, at least in formal writing.

Only a fool would fight custom with grammar.

Montaigne

turn on

Turn on is a conversational expression for something we get a kick out of. It is not necessarily sexual but usually is.

twee

Baby-talk rarely becomes normal usage but this happened to *twee*. It was to begin with probably a babyish way of saying 'sweet' and then became an informal word for something that is coy or arch. But dictionaries now admit *twee* into standard English.

U

U and **Non-U English**
See **class language**

UN acronyms

The United Nations has given birth to a whole group of *acronyms* – words made out of the initial letters of other words. Some have become words in their own right and are spelt with an initial capital letter followed by small letters: *Unesco* (United Nations Educational, Scientific and Cultural Organization), *Unicef* (United Nations International Children's Emergency Fund), *Unrra* (United Nations Relief and Rehabilitation Administration). Others are pronounced as a word but are spelt in capitals: *UNCTAD* (United Nations Conference on Trade and Development), *UNDRO* (United Nations Disaster Relief Organization). Note: An apostrophe is not used after *United Nations*: 'United Nations personnel'.

un- words

For over a thousand years, *un-* has been prefixed to words in English to give them an opposite meaning. Over the centuries so many *un-* words have accumulated that no dictionary can list them all. So if you think of a useful *un-* word and cannot find it in a dictionary, that's no reason for not using it. In any case, many writers invent *un-* words to suit themselves. Kingsley Amis described a woman with '*unabundant* brown hair'; the *New Statesman* came up with *unpublicity* about something that had escaped the attention of the media; critics call bad comedians or comedy films *unfunny*; in sociology jargon, the unpleasant word 'slum' is avoided by substituting '*unfit* housing'; a fashion writer described a dress that was a real 'turn off' as *unsexy*. When it is used intelligently to evoke an idea, *un-* is part of the continuing creativity of English.

unconditional or **unconditioned†**

Dictionaries show both these words as meaning not subject to conditions: 'an *unconditional* surrender'. But *unconditioned* is now often used in a much more interesting way to mean a natural unfettered open response, free from the old backlog of associations, influences and unquestioned handed-down beliefs: 'If you look at this in an *unconditioned* way you will see new solutions.'

unconscious or **subconscious**

See **subconscious**

under or **under-**

In most cases a hyphen is unnecessary: underachieve, underact, undercarriage, undercover, undercut, underdeveloped, undermanned, understudy, etc. Among the few words that usually take a hyphen are: *under-secretary* and *under-sexed*. When in doubt spell *under* words without a hyphen.

under or **in the circumstances**

A few pedants still argue that *circumstances* are 'around' us, so *under* the circumstances is illogical and only *in* the circumstances will do. Fowler dismissed the rule as stupid. Language, created in the daily illogical lives of people, is not logical and it is equally good English to do something *under the circumstances* or *in the circumstances*.

The syntax may go to hell but what I'm aiming for is the true conversational tone of one man talking to another.

Alistair Cooke, *Sunday Times*

undue

Many people are not sure what *undue* means and it has become a pompous word slipped in to sound important: 'There is no cause for *undue* alarm', 'It does not require *undue* intelligence to understand this.' *Undue* means not yet due or not suitable and there are few occasions when it is required. To avoid sounding like a stuffed shirt, do not use *undue* unless it is really necessary, which will not be often.

uneatable or **inedible**

See **inedible**

unequivocal or **unequivocable****

Unequivocal means there is no doubt and that something is absolutely clear: 'We have to accept this *unequivocal* decision.' Even though you hear it sometimes in the best of circles, *unequivocable* is not in any dictionary, because there is no such word.

unexceptionable or **unexceptional**

Often mixed up. When something is *unexceptionable* no

faults can be found with it: 'He put forward a plan that everyone considered *unexceptionable.*' *Unexceptional* means ordinary or commonplace (the opposite of 'exceptional'): 'The bill was too much for such an *unexceptional* meal.'

unilateral

A word much loved by politicians and diplomats, who talk about *unilateral* disarmament, *unilateral* decisions, etc., when they could just as easily say 'one-sided'. There's no need for the rest of us to jump on that linguistic bandwagon.

Let us not shrink from using the short expressive phrase even when it is conversational.

Winston Churchill

uninterested or **disinterested**
See **disinterested**
unique

Unique means the only one of its kind and is a so-called 'absolute' word, like *true*. The rules of the game are we must never write or say *very unique*** or *quite unique**

because there are no degrees of uniqueness. *Almost unique* is all right because it suggests that there are very few like it. Yet most people are happy with 'absolutely true' or even 'very true' and as good a writer as Charlotte Bronte wrote 'a very *unique* child'. If you decide to keep to the rules, you will use the word *rare*, except when something is truly *unique*.

unisex language

Some *unisex language* is obligatory under the Sex Discrimination Act in Britain, because it is now illegal to advertise jobs which specify either a man or a woman. *Unisex* words have been demanded by the feminist movement, and among younger people, both men and women, there seems to be a feeling that the time has come to at least reduce the masculine bias in English. Different aspects of this are dealt with under **everybody, chairman, humankind, Ms, sexist language, spokesperson.**

... for the benefit and helpe of Ladies, Gentlewomen, or any other unskilfull persons.
> Robert Cawdrey, Foreword to the first
> English dictionary, 1604

universally

Universally means everywhere or by everyone and it makes a nonsense of the word to say 'She is *universally* liked' when all we mean is she is liked by all her friends.

unmanageable or **unmanagable****

Unmanageable.

unmistakable or **unmistakeable****

Unmistakable.

unmovable or **unmoveable****

Unmovable.

unparalleled or **unparallelled****

Double the first *l* but not the second: *unparalleled* is correct. See **parallel**

unprecedented

Pronounce it 'unPRESSsedented' not 'unPREESsedented'.

unreadable

Does not mean the same as 'illegible'. 'Illegible' is a fact – something is impossible to read because, for example, the handwriting is so bad or the print is too blurred. *Unreadable* is a matter of opinion – something is too dull and heavy-going to read. This book is certainly not illegible and I hope you do not find it *unreadable*.

unsalable** or **unsaleable**

Unsaleable.

unshakable** or **unshakeable**

Unshakeable.

unsympathetic†

When we say someone is *unsympathetic* we could mean they lack sympathy for people who are suffering or that they're not pleasant people to be with. Make sure that the way you say it or the context makes it clear what is meant. See **sympathetic**

until or **till**

Interchangeable, although *until* could be considered more formal but in no way more correct.

update

There are still people who don't like this word. It's here to stay as standard English because it's shorter and quicker than 'bring up to date'.

upon or **on**

See **on**

uptight†

Most dictionaries give two meanings: tense and nervous ('She's so *uptight* about her driving test') or starchy and conventional ('He's so *uptight* with his daughter's boyfriends'). *Uptight* is used the second way in America and more and more often that way in the UK as well. *Uptight* is also used with a sexual connotation to mean sexually repressed and inhibited. Dictionaries sometimes treat *uptight* as colloquial (although not slang) but it's such a useful vivid word that it has become standard English.

Words are, of course, the most powerful drug used by mankind.

> Rudyard Kipling, used as headline in advertisement
> for the *Times Literary Supplement*

upward adjustment and **upward movement**

Some politicians and economists feel that an *upward*

adjustment in prices or an *upward movement* in the number of unemployed are less harsh ways of saying we have to pay more and there are more people on the dole. *Upward adjustment* and *upward movement* are smokescreen expressions.

US or **States** or **America**

See **States**

usage or **use**

Usage is not the same as use: usage means the way in which something is used – good *usage*, rough *usage*, efficient *usage*, etc. We should not write 'The *usage* of swimming pools has increased.' The proper word there is *use*. Eric Partridge called his book on the English language *Usage and Abusage*, and similarly I have written *usage* in this book to refer to the *way* English is used.

used to

No problem when it's a straightforward statement: 'I *used to* walk to work.' Problems start when it's negative or asking a question. Strictly speaking, we should say 'I used not to walk to work', although most of us are happier with 'I did not use to walk to work', which a few people reject as almost illiterate. For asking a question, a few people would insist on 'Used you not to walk to work?', which sounds as starchy as a wing-collar. 'Didn't you use to walk to work?' is the only natural way of asking. *Didn't use to* and *didn't you use to?* are both considered good standard English by Oxford authorities. The correct contracted forms are: *usedn't to* and *didn't use to*. *Usen't to* and *didn't used to*, often seen, are errors.

user-friendly

User-friendly was first used about computer systems that lead users along by easy steps without complicated language. The words have since become extended to cover any machine designed to make it easy to understand and operate. *User-friendly* is a linguistic recognition of the near-human abilities of computers and robots.

No dictionary of a living tongue ever can be perfect, since while it is hastening to publication, some words are budding and some falling away.

Samuel Johnson, Preface to the *Dictionary*

V

value-judgements†

People talk about *value-judgements* without always being clear what they mean. A *value-judgement* is based on a subjective assessment of whether something is good or bad, social or antisocial, etc. If we say that experiments on human embryos are wrong because they degrade human life, that is a *value-judgement*. *Value-judgement* often carries a pejorative implication ('That's just a value-judgement'), suggesting that we should avoid a subjective point of view. This fails to recognize that absolute objectivity is beyond the reach of most of us, so nearly all judgements are, to some extent, *value-judgements*.

vasectomy

Twenty-five years ago the *Shorter Oxford Dictionary* did not include this word, presumably because it was considered too specialized. Now *vasectomy* is in general use because the surgical operation it describes, which permanently sterilizes a man, has become so much more common.

verbal or oral

See **oral**

verbosity

We have all come across compulsive talkers, people who are so nervous that they wear out everyone they meet with a deluge of words. That's *verbosity* and it's almost like an illness. It's the same in writing, when people bolster their confidence or self-esteem with 'in relation to', 'with reference to', 'in respect of', 'it is appreciated that', 'it is considered advisable to bring to your attention' and hundreds of other stodgy cotton wool expressions.

Every time we avoid *verbosity* we increase the chance that someone will read what we've written. See **pleonasm** and **tautology**

> *Zounds! I was never so bethump'd with words,*
> *Since first I call'd my brother's father dad.*
> Shakespeare, *King John*

very

We have been taught that *very* is used too often and some people who pride themselves on the way they write say they are '*most* pleased', '*so* happy', '*extremely* grateful' and so on. *Very* is overused and we should be careful about that, which does not mean that we can never be '*very* angry' or '*very* much in love'. To say that we should never use *very* is very stupid.

viable

In biology, an organism that is *viable* is one that can survive independently, outside the mother. It is a legitimate extension of this to talk of a subsidiary company being viable, that is able to keep going without the support of the parent company. From this usage it became fashionable to use *viable* to mean feasible or workable ('a *viable* proposition'). Though this usage is disliked by a few people, because the word has lost its roots, it has come to stay and is now recognized as a valid meaning of *viable* by the COD and LD. *Economically viable* is such a standard phrase now for something that will pay its way, that it would be difficult to avoid using it.

Words and expressions will be forced into use in spite of all the exertions of all the writers in the world.
> Noah Webster, *An American Dictionary of*
> *the English Language*

vibes†

To get bad *vibes* from something or somebody means to have an intuitive feeling that something is not right. This use of *vibes*, an abbreviation for 'vibrations', is an unconscious recognition of extra-sensory perception, implying that a message is coming across in a way we cannot define. No longer slang, *vibes* has moved up to colloquial usage in recent dictionaries.

vintage†

Vintage, of course, properly describes wine from a particular year. Its extended use, for anything from the past that is particularly good and enduring, or for a specially successful year, has become general: 'a *vintage* performance', 'a *vintage* year for breaking records'. By general consent a *vintage car* is one made between 1917 or 1919 and 1930 (a *veteran* car is one made before 1916, according to some authorities, and before 1905 according to others).

violin

See **fiddle**

virtuoso

The proper plural for this Italian word is *virtuosi* but *virtuosos* is also acceptable in English and more usual.

vitamin

You can choose whether you take 'vitt-amins' or 'vite-amins'. Both pronunciations are generally regarded as correct, unless you are a BBC announcer, in which case you are asked to say 'vitt-amins'.

vulgar

All the four-letter *Lady Chatterley* words are classified as *vulgar* in dictionaries, perhaps because they don't feel they can go so far as to call them 'obscene'. Yet in other ways vulgar is a harmless enough word, used for the ordinary English name for a plant or animal rather than the Latin name. And there is nothing indecent about *vulgar fractions*. The pejorative meanings of *vulgar* (which comes from the Latin *vulgus* meaning the common people) derive from believing that the taste and style of the great mass of people must be rather nasty. See **dirty words** and **four-letter words**

> *Here are a few of the unpleasant'st words*
> *That ever blotted paper!*
> Shakespeare, *Merchant of Venice*

wake or **waken**

'I *wake* (up) every morning at 7 o'clock'; 'I *woke* (up) during the night'; 'I was *woken* (up) at 7 o'clock.' You can say or write 'wake', 'woke', 'woken', *or* 'wake up', etc. *Waken* is another alternative: 'I *waken* every morning at 7 o'clock'; 'I *wakened* during the night'; 'I was *wakened* at 7 o'clock.' *Wake* is more usual now and easier to use in its different forms. See **awake**

walkabout

First used in Australia for the ritual wandering in the bush by an aborigine. In recent years *walkabout* has been adopted in the UK and US as a descriptive easygoing word for an informal stroll among the crowds by royalty or a president.

All I need is a catchy phrase that anybody can understand.
Irving Berlin

walkie-talkie

Dictionaries now classify this babyish expression, for a hand-held radio receiver and transmitter, as standard English.

walkman

Walkman is a *Sony* trademark. It is included in some dictionaries as the general word for *any* small cassette-player with lightweight earphones that go with a faraway look on someone's face, as they walk, jog, shop in supermarkets, or do whatever else they don't want to think about.

wanna***

Even the most permissive writer on English usage must give thumbs down to 'I *wanna* coffee'. *Wanna*, *kinda* and *sorta* are sloppy slangy variants of 'want a', 'kind of', and 'sort of'.

Farewell, farewell to my beloved language,
Once English, now a vile orangutanguage.
Ogden Nash, *Laments for a Dying Language*

was or **were**

See **if I was** or **if I were**

wastage or **waste**

Some people think *wastage* is a posh word for *waste*. But in fact it has a different meaning. A *waste* of something is when it's used uselessly: 'Dripping taps are a *waste* of water.' *Wastage* is loss through legitimate use or natural causes: 'In very hot weather there is a *wastage* of thousands of gallons from reservoirs through evaporation.'

we'd

See **contracted forms**

weekend or **week-end**

Week end started as two words, then became hyphenated (*week-end* – 1976 COD) and is now standard as *one* word: *weekend* (1982 COD), which will please the French who have been writing *le weekend* for years.

well or **well-**

Usually well-: well-known, well-being, well-spoken, well-to-do, well-thought-of, well-tried, well-timed.

wench

This Falstaffian word once meant a serving-woman. Somehow it has survived, out-of-date though it is; there are still men who affectionately call women *wenches*. Some women like it while others find it offensive. And there are 'olde worlde' restaurants on the tourist circuit that call waitresses *serving wenches*, implying bosomy and saucy.

west

See **north, south, east** and **west**

wet

Who first called the more moderate members of Margaret Thatcher's government *wet*? And does the idea come from *wet behind the ears*, meaning inexperienced, immature and feeble? Whatever the answers, *wet* has become a derogatory description of a right-wing politician with middle-of-the-road policies. It belongs to Thatcherite history.

wh-

In Scotland and Ireland you still hear the *h* pronounced: 'hwat', 'hwen', 'hwether', etc. (what, when, whether). It used to be a middle-class 'refinement' to 'hwat', 'hwen',

etc. in England as well but this is now dropping out. As far back as the early 1920s, Henry Wyld, an authority on the history of English, considered the 'hw' sound in southern English artificial and affected.

what are or **what is**

No problem about 'What we need *is* more money.' Grammarians argue that we should also say 'What we need is more houses for people to live in', because *what* stands for 'the thing' which is singular. That's as may be but 'What we need *are* more houses ...' sounds more natural and is the usual way of putting it. When the word relating to *what* is plural (as in 'more houses' above), both *are* and *is* are acceptable, which is also the view taken in *Plain Words*, the guide to English for the civil service.

which or **that** or **who**

See **that**

which are or **which is**

'Which of the five books *are* best?' means which two, three or four of the books are best. 'Which of the five books *is* best?' means which *one* of them is best.

while or **awhile**

Either 'He remained there awhile' or '... *for a* while', but *not* 'for awhile'.

while or **whilst**

Interchangeable. Both words properly relate to time: 'She phoned *while* you were out.' Both words are also used as an alternative for 'although': '*While* I understand your problem, I don't think it is serious.' There is nothing wrong with this but it can sometimes lead to confusion: '*While* she knows nothing about it, I expect she'll cope quite well' (the implication is that if she knew more, she'd make a hash of it!). Use 'although' instead.

whisky or **whiskey**

Whisky in Scotland and Canada – *whiskey* in Ireland and the US.

whites

We refer to *white* people or *black* people or *whites* or *blacks*. *Non-white* is used occasionally but it can give offence. See **Caucasian** and **racist words**

whiz-kid

Slang to begin with but now standard English in *LD* (colloquial in *COD*). It should be used only about *young* people who are brilliantly successful or clever, although it belongs more to the 1960s. *Whiz-* or *whizz-*, by the way.

Slang is language which takes off its coat, spits on its hands and goes to work.

Carl Sandburg

who or **whom**

Some writers believe that *whom* will be as dead as the dodo in perhaps twenty years. Others take a pride in switching between *who* and *whom* according to the grammarians' rules. So concerned are they, that even good writers sometimes force in *whom* when *who* is correct: 'A creature *whom* we pretend is here already' (E.M. Forster), where *who* should have been used.

If you want to get it right, try dividing the sentence into two and see whether you use 'he' or 'him' (or 'she' or 'her'). If it's him, use *whom* in the original sentence, otherwise use *who*. Two examples:

1 The man *whom* I saw yesterday: The man. I saw *him* yesterday.

2 The man *who* I think was here yesterday: The man. I think *he* was here yesterday.

If you prefer to take it easy, use *who* right across the board except for *to whom, from whom, with whom* and *for whom* (at least in writing), but expect to be picked up for it occasionally. *Whom* can sound a little stuffy in speech: '*Whom* shall I send it to?' which although correct is less usual than '*Who* shall I send it to?' But it has not yet dropped out in writing and some people who care about English still prefer to use *who* and *whom* in the orthodox way.

If sticking grimly to all the rules of grammar makes you sound like a pompous pedant, you are a pompous pedant.
William Safire in the *New York Times*

whodunit

Still current, a *whodunit* is as neat a name as any for a book, play or film based on a detective or murder story.

whoever or **whomever**

'Whomever is it for?' is correct English, if you don't mind sounding on your best grammatical behaviour. The *Oxford Guide to English Usage* considered *whomever* is 'rather stilted' and recommended that *whoever* should now be used in all cases. Here's an example of everyday usage of English superseding formal grammar. See **who** or **whom**

who's or **whose**

Who's is the contracted form of 'who is' or 'who has': 'Who's there?' *Whose* always relates to possession: '*Whose* book is it?'

will or **shall**

See **shall**

wine language (or 'winespeak')

The *wine game* is played out at dinner-tables, in restaurants and at wine-tastings. In order to keep your end up you have to know some of the language: wine doesn't smell good – it has a *good nose*; wine is *big* or *meaty* rather than powerful; *round* or *velvety* rather than smooth; *dumb* rather than nothing special; *flabby* rather than tasteless; *corked* rather than 'off'. The best wines are *elegant* or *well-bred*. Wine can have *finesse*, a *finish*, *character* and can be *forthcoming*, *earthy*, *complex*, or *sensuous*. Those descriptions are all part of the established vocabulary of the *wine game*.

It's a Naïve Domestic Burgundy without Any Breeding. But I Think You'll be Amused by its Presumption.

James Thurber, *Men, Women and Dogs*

wireless

See **radio**

-wise

Wise has been tacked on to words for centuries and everyone accepts *likewise*, *crosswise*, *clockwise*, *otherwise* and other well-established *-wise* words. But some people object to *-wise* being added to other words – it is '… ungrammatical, unnecessary and ugly, to be avoided by all but the most insensitive' according to one writer. Those are hard words about a linguistic additive that has been used in English since before the 14th century. Admittedly

-wise has become overused jargon, but that doesn't mean it is not useful sometimes: *careerwise* is quicker than 'in relation to my career', *engineeringwise** neater than 'with regard to the engineering aspects', *moneywise* more direct than 'as far as money is concerned'.

If you use *-wise* too often it becomes a linguistic gimmick. But occasionally *-wise* added to a word can say something quickly and effectively for you.

with

'What shall I do it *with*?' is perfectly good English. See **prepositions at end of sentences**

wog

See **racist words**

woman

Successful professional women are often relaxed about using *woman* to describe themselves or other women, especially if they regard *girl* as belittling for any woman over 18. We hear about 'The *Woman* of the Year', 'a distinguished *woman* barrister'; the BBC called the TV series about Flora Robson, Janet Vaughan, Barbara Wootton and others '*Women* of our Century'. Back in 1973, Margaret Thatcher made the mistake of the century when she said 'I don't think there will be a *woman* prime minister in my lifetime.'

Yet in spite of those examples, men are often hesitant about calling a woman a *woman* in case it offends her. Perhaps this is a hangover from the idea that *woman* is a degraded word in the way that *man* never is ('She's just a common woman'). Children are brought up to hear 'Say *Thank you* to the *lady*' and so on.

Nor is *female* a safe alternative, since it often carries with it a derogatory implication: 'So I said to this *female* ....' There is no reliable advice in this uneasy linguistic situation as we hover between offending a 'lady' by calling her a *woman* or sounding genteel or even ridiculous sometimes by saying *lady*. See **girl, lady** and **Ms**

womankind or **womenkind**

Womankind is better as it corresponds to 'mankind'.

wonderous or **wondrous**

Wondrous. See **disasterous**

working class

It would venture into deep waters to define *working class* in the 21st century. The term has lost its social, economic and cultural cohesion. People in traditionally working-class occupations might now live in the same street as people working in banks, etc. They might be earning more money, travel to faraway places on holiday, have children at universities. There could still be certain characteristics of lifestyle, social attitudes and manner of speaking, but *working class* can no longer be defined clearly. See **class**

world-class

World-class became a popular term in sport during the 1980s, for someone at the highest level of performance by world standards. *World-class* is now extended to all fields: for example, the *Independent* has carried a feature on how Britain could get 'world-class schools'.

Is thought available in any other form than words – aren't the words themselves the thought, as it thinks itself into existence?

Robert Robinson, in a letter to the BBC

worthwhile or **worth-while** or **worth while**

'The experiment was *worth* while' (two words) but 'It was a *worthwhile* (or *worth-while*) experiment.'

would or **should**

See **should**

write

It's good English in the US to say 'I'll write you about it' but in the UK it should be 'I'll write *to* you about it.'

writer or **author**

As the curtain falls on the last scene of the first night of a play, it is traditional for the audience to call out *Author*! *Author*! Nevertheless the tendency now is for authors to call themselves *writers*. *The Society of Authors* was founded in 1884 but the more recent association is called *The Writers' Guild*. The same person now will often write a book, a play, a film and for television, which is why *writer* is taking over as the more usual word – although not all *authors* will agree. *Authoress* is not used now as *author* (when it is used) covers both sexes.

X

xerox

Xerox is the trademark for the pioneer photocopying machine using the xerographic process. The accolade of success is that *xerox* (like *hoover* for *any* vacuum cleaner) is often used now for any kind of photocopying: 'Will you *xerox* this please?'

Y

yeses or **yesses**

'When the vote was taken there were ten yeses' (not yesses*).

Yiddish and **Hebrew**

See **Hebrew**

Yinglish†

Included in *LD* (as informal English) although disdained by *COD*, *Yinglish* is the English used by a number of Jews, particularly in New York. During the last century, especially in the first two decades, nearly two million Jews emigrated to the US, leaving behind the poverty and persecution of Eastern Europe, and New York became the largest 'Jewish' city in the world. Yiddish was their main language and as it merged with English, *Yinglish* was born. Many colourful *Yinglish* expressions have become so much a part of English that we almost forget their origin: 'I should have such luck!', 'It shouldn't happen to a dog', 'I need it like a hole in the head', 'It's OK by me', 'Get lost!' But ... 'Enough is enough already'! See **Hebrew, goy, kosher, nosh**

Yinglish ... is a rich source of vocabulary and idiom flowing into the central sea of English.

Philip Howard, *For liking Yinglish, I should apologise?* (in *The Times*)

you and I or **you and me**
See **I** or **me**

you know
Perhaps *you know* or *y'know* are used too often in conversation and on television as unnecessary 'fillers'. No doubt they give whoever is speaking time to think of what to say next. But a pause would be just as good.

yours or **your's**
Never *your's*.***

Z

zany

Contrary to what some people believe, *zany* is not slang but good standard English going back to the 16th century, when it was used for a 'stooge' playing up to a clown. *Zany* is still a good word for anyone or anything that seems crazy.

Zen

A form of Buddhism (*Zen Buddhism*) that uses the discipline of detachment and meditation to arrive at true understanding and enlightenment. *Zen* is now used sometimes to describe an intuitive non-intellectual unconditioned approach: some years ago a bestselling book was called *Zen and the Art of Motorcycle Maintenance*.

zenith and **nadir**

See **nadir**

Zip code

The name for US postal code (capital Z, small c).

There can never be a moment when language truly stands still, any more than there is a pause in the ever-blazing thoughts of men.

Wilhelm von Humboldt (in 1836)

Thanks

This book owes much to lexicographers and to other writers on the English language. Below are listed the principal dictionaries and books to which I have turned for cross-checks and for different opinions on aspects of English usage. The fact that I have not always followed the same line does not diminish my gratitude to the writers and editors for the signposts they have left on the path along which I travelled:

Broadcast English (A. Lloyd James, BBC 1930). *Bullock Report on the Teaching of English* (HMSO 1975). *The Changing English Language* (Brian Foster, Macmillan). *Class* (Jilly Cooper, Eyre Methuen). *The Complete Plain Words* (Sir Ernest Gowers and Sir Bruce Fraser, HMSO). *A Concise Dictionary of Correct English* (B.A. Phythian, Hodder & Stoughton). *A Dictionary of Slang and Unconventional English* (Eric Partridge, Routledge & Kegan Paul). *Grammar* (Tony Sullivan, National Extension College). *Language Change: Progress or Decay?* (Jean Aitchison, Fontana). *Longman Dictionary of the English Language*. *The Loom of Language* (Frederick Bodmer, George Allen & Unwin). *Modern English Usage* (H.W. Fowler, Oxford University Press).

OXFORD DICTIONARIES:
The Oxford English Dictionary. *The Shorter Oxford English Dictionary*. *The Concise Oxford Dictionary*. *The Oxford Dictionary of English Etymology* (C.T. Onions). *The Oxford Dictionary for Writers and Editors*. *The Oxford Guide to English Usage* (E.S.C. Weiner, Oxford University Press).

The Penguin Dictionary of Troublesome Words (Bill Bryson, Penguin Books). *Roget's Thesaurus* (Susan M. Lloyd, Longman). *A Short History of English* (H.C. Wyld, John Murray). *The Slanguage of Sex* (Brigid McConville & John Shearlaw, Macdonald). *The Spoken Word* (Robert Burchfield, BBC). *The State of the Language* (Leonard Michaels & Christopher Ricks, University of California). *Usage and Abusage* (Eric Partridge, Penguin Books). *Who Cares About English Usage?* (David Crystal, Penguin Books). *Wordpower* (Edward de Bono, Pierrot Publishing).